THE
SPIRITUAL LIFE OF
ARCHBISHOP
MARTINEZ

Cross and Crown Series of Spirituality

LITERARY EDITOR

Reverend Jordan Aumann, O.P., S.T.D.

NUMBER 33

THE
SPIRITUAL LIFE OF
ARCHBISHOP
MARTINEZ

Joseph G. Trevino, M.Sp.S.

TRANSLATED BY

Sister Mary St. Daniel Tarrant, B.V.M.

B. Herder Book Co.

ST. LOUIS AND LONDON

A translation of
Monseñor Martinez, Semblanza de su Vida Interior
by J. G. Treviño, Missionary of the Holy Spirit,
Editorial "La Cruz," Mexico, D. F., 1956

IMPRIMATUR
✠ Joseph Cardinal Ritter
Archbishop of St. Louis
September 2, 1966

DEDICATED TO
OUR LADY OF GUADALUPE
LIGHT OF MY DAYS
IN MEXICO

The Translator

FOREWORD

To write the biography of a man is something like translating a book. To translate is to change into one's own tongue something written in another; and this involves enormous difficulties. It presupposes a perfect knowledge of both languages. To express the difficulty of making a good translation, the Italians say: *Traduttore, tradittore.*

Now, a man is a book written by God himself. Each creature is the translation, in his lifetime, of a word pronounced by God eternally. What an excellent translation God has made of his eternal discourse in the marvels of creation! For one who knows how to read it, the heavens truly chant the glory of God, and each creature is a magnificent psalm composed by the Holy Spirit.

And we may also point out a most perfect translation which God made of his own substantial Word. To translate that Word, that living discourse which God pronounces in time, is to know all, to possess all, because it is to possess eternal life. "Now this is everlasting life, that they may know thee, the only true God, and him whom thou hast sent, Jesus Christ" (John 17:3). Only God could translate in that sublime, divine way, because only he knows and commands fully both his own language and that of creatures. "And that which contains all things has knowledge of the voice" (Wis. 1:7). Jesus is the living, perfect biography of God.

All proportion guarded, we, too, translate ourselves and we translate others when we write a biography; but the difficulty lies not only in what is inherent in the relation of both languages, but in something far more momentous, since it is an attempt to interpret a man in what is strictly his own and most personal to him. A biography is not the simple, chronological

vii

enumeration of memorable dates in a man's life, to tell us the place and the date of his birth, the most noteworthy events of his life, and finally the place and the date of his death. This is history, and history often cannot hold the interest, except of professional researchers.

Biography enters the secret domain of the soul, hidden in great part from the gaze of others, and even from the subject himself. And if one is writing about a Christian and a priest, the difficulty increases, because it is not only the psychological mystery that one must know in order to draw a human portrait, but also the obscure, mysterious ways of grace.

The book you are holding in your hand is a biography, the translation of a man. It tries to tell what God, grace and nature jointly wrote in a book that we knew. Those three forces, combined, and working for seventy-five years in different times and places and in the most diverse circumstances from June 9, 1881, to February 9, 1956, could write so much for the story of the man and especially of God's role in his life.

How many times we saw that book! How many times we looked through the pages without understanding, or without entirely understanding. And how many times we wish, now that it is set apart from the shelves of life, that we had read and understood it better! There was need for someone to translate it as perfectly as possible and put the volume into our hands to tell us in our language the magnificent story of a life.

The life of Archbishop Louis Martínez displays surpassingly rich gifts of nature, gifts so numerous and so great that we must admit that seldom are they joined in one individual man alone: broad, deep intelligence; strong, determined will; brilliant, creative imagination; ready, elevated and persuasive speech; a magnanimous, loyal, understanding heart; and even a refreshing, engaging sense of humor that sometimes flowed out in a cascade of laughter. As for the world of sanctifying grace, as well as his priestly activity, few could read those secret, invisible pages, and those few often read in an incomplete or poorly interpreted fashion.

Father Treviño's purpose in writing this biography of Archbishop Martínez was to translate him for us so that we might understand him. No one is so fitted to undertake this arduous yet welcome task. He was acquainted with the Archbishop for many, many years. He knew him as seminarian, as priest, as bishop. He knew him outwardly, because he lived with him for a long time; and he knew him within, because he was his confessor and friend.

A friend, I said, and a friend in the entire extension of the word. For the Archbishop friendship was a real virtue. He not only was grateful for it, he valued it and he knew how to select as close friends those like himself or those whom he had made to his own image and likeness. This is one of the powers that reveal the greatness of a man: to know how to establish around him, through the sheer force of his personality and convictions, persons who resemble him. The truly great man—Archbishop Martínez was such—does not permit himself to be assimilated; he assimilates. We may well say that when anyone was a friend of Archbishop Martínez it was because His Excellency had impressed himself upon that person.

Aside from this, there were marked likenesses between the Archbishop and Father Treviño which explain that intimate friendship; although there were great differences which also explain it, if it is true that friends must be sufficiently alike to understand each other and sufficiently different to complement each other.

Both possessed an exquisite sensibility denoting the artist, the mystic and the saint, a sensibility never exaggerated but always subordinated to faith and reason. Both were of an almost painful shyness, dissembling and concealing their affections; both were devoted to the study of mysticism and, by the will of God and the force of circumstances, frequently called upon to apply this mystical knowledge in the direction of souls.

Furthermore, Archbishop Martínez was as open as a cloudless sky; simple and guileless, in spite of his reputation as diplomat—a title he habitually repudiated. The other was more closed, like the book of seven seals; through a refined modesty he did not wish to open the treasure of his soul, which he esteemed as little or nothing; complex with a complexity more apparent than real, which suggests a depth that we do not penetrate at once; devoted to duty. Yet they are counterpart souls, souls belonging to God and entirely surrendered to him, although in different conditions. This very thing, more than anything else, entitles Father Treviño to give us his translation of Archbishop Martínez.

✠Fernando Ruiz
Archbishop of Yucatán

AUTHOR'S PREFACE

Much has been written about Archbishop Martínez and much more will be written as time clarifies and exalts his colossal figure. His personality presents varied aspects, like a diamond of multiple facets; hence, he may be studied as philosopher, theologian, educator, superior, sociologist, sacred orator, writer, poet, spiritual director, humorist. But perhaps there is one aspect that has remained in the shadows until now, in spite of its paramount importance: it is the interior man, his spiritual life, his intimate relations with God; in a word, it is the mystic.

He is a mystic, not in the sense given the term by those who call any religious exaltation "mysticism," but in its genuine, theological meaning. He was not a speculative mystic, as are so many who write about what they have studied in authors or observed in other souls; he was an experimental mystic, one who speaks and writes of what has happened to him personally, in the style of St. Teresa, or better, of St. John of the Cross.

Since grace does not destroy nature but is grafted upon it, we cannot study the *man of God* without studying the *man,* that is to say, his temperament, his character, his psychology, his atavisms, the factors that influenced his formation, and so on. In treating of such delicate matters, we shall let Archbishop Martínez speak with his own words, wherever possible, while we limit ourselves to giving explanations and pertinent comments.

Aside from this, if this work has any merit, it is due to the unpublished writings of the Archbishop and to the fact that we are speaking of what we ourselves witnessed in person. Therefore, pardon us for speaking so frequently in the first person; it is not a thoughtless conceit, but only the desire of giving greater interest and credibility to the narrative. It is not the same thing to say: "They relate that," as to say: "I saw him; I myself was present." We hope that fifty-two years of intimate contact may give some validity to our statements.

J. G. Treviño, M.Sp.S.

CONTENTS

CONTENTS

CHAPTER I

En Route

RESTING UPON the slopes of the Cantabrian Sea, Ballota hides its cottages among luxurious apple orchards. The entire landscape is a gamut of lively colors: the azure of an ever limpid sky, the deep blue of the sea, the dark green of the apple trees, the bright red of their fruit, the dull green of the olive groves, the delicate green of the meadows. Day and night the ceaseless clamor of the waves is heard as they keep dashing against the slopes and, conquered, recede topped with a gauze of whitest foam.

Among the homes of Ballota our interest lies especially in a cottage, two stories high, with an exterior stairway and devoid of any fence, for the whole village is like one large family. This is the home of the Martínez family.

One of its members, Rosendo, still very young, is dreaming of going to America. Can it be the spirit of the conquistador inherited from the vassals of Isabel the Catholic and of Philip II? Can it be the eagerness for growth that suffocates them, as it were, in the narrow confines of a small village? Spaniards frequently emigrated to America, especially to Mexico, not as adventurers or transients, but to establish themselves there, to make a fortune with honest work, and frequently to marry a Mexican woman and thus found a Mexican home and a creole family.

So it happened with the young Rosendo. His dreams were realized; he came to Mexico. He engaged in business and agriculture and, by dint of labor and honesty, he rose to the position of manager of the rich hacienda of Molinos de Caballero,

1

strategically situated on the boundaries of three States—
Michoacán, Mexico and Querétaro—but which belongs officially to the State of Michoacán in the Archdiocese of Morelia
and the parish of Tlalpujahua.

Rosendo, in young manhood, prepossessing in appearance,
with a leisurely position, could have led a dissipated life, but
it was just the opposite, for his strong Asturian faith and his
solitude far away from his loved ones brought him near to God.
Along this road he reached a union with God by no means
ordinary, which cannot but be surprising in view of the circumstances and the time in which he lived. He practiced mental
prayer, every Friday he fasted, he communicated almost daily—
a highly significant fact in an age when the decree of St. Pius
X on daily Communion was still far away.

There is one detail very significant in its implications: the
day on which Rosendo contracted marriage was Friday. Anyone
would have dispensed himself from his practice of voluntary
mortification on such a festive occasion. But Rosendo did not
want to break his resolution and on that day he fasted as on any
other Friday.

At that time, in the year 1880, the vicar of the hacienda was
Father Casimir Rodríguez, an exemplary priest. His young sister, whom everyone called by the diminutive, Ramoncita, lived
in his house. And she merited that affectionate diminutive. She
was of such a sweet character, so mild, so gentle, so tender-
hearted that she captivated everybody. These qualities were
complemented by a spirited disposition. Physically she was of
fine features, a delicately dark complexion and genteel bearing.

Rosendo, the administrator of the hacienda, and Ramoncita,
the vicar's little sister, became acquainted, fell in love and were
married. They established their home in a cottage across the
way from the great house of the hacienda; a home where all
was sweetness and peace.

Adjoining the house was an orchard with fruit trees native

to temperate lands: peach, pear and plum. Nearby a river glided gently on its course; the air was bright and clear and no sound was heard but the unceasing murmur of the waters. A little farther on, the river, torrential and magnificent, dashed down into a deep glen; it was the waterfall of Tepuxtepec.

The joy of that home reached a climax when a boy was born on June 9, 1881. Father Casimir baptized the child, giving him the name of Louis Gonzaga María. Before his birth his parents had consecrated him to the Blessed Virgin.

Nothing was lacking to the happiness of that family. But how inscrutable are the designs of God! It might seem as if it pleased him to destroy happiness, but only to construct upon those ruins a happiness that is eternal.

The infant was scarcely eleven days old, when a sudden illness carried off the father in the prime of life. Ramoncita, with her infant, again took up her abode with her brother, the vicar. She concentrated the treasures of her heart's tenderness upon her son. Her brother constituted himself adoptive father of the boy and with his pure, manly affection he tried to fill the void that orphanhood left in the child's heart. Therefore, when the child began to stammer his first words, he would call him "Papa Mirito."

An incident illustrates Father Casimir's deep affection for Louis. It was market day on the hacienda, that is, the day on which the surrounding merchants came there to offer their wares. While passing among the booths, Louis asked his mother to buy him a toy that had greatly attracted his attention. Ramoncita, through fear of being a heavier financial burden for her brother, tried to convince Louis that he should forget the toy because it was very expensive and "Papa Mirito" did not have the money to spend for it. But the child began to cry and was still crying when they arrived home.

Father Casimir noticed it, and as he could not endure the boy's tears, he called Ramoncita and inquired the cause. When she explained the matter, the priest said: "No, Ramoncita, we must buy whatever the child wants, whether cheap or expensive."

Louis, in an adjoining room, caught those words and he kept them as an invincible weapon. An occasion soon presented itself. He asked Ramoncita to buy something for him which seemed unnecessary to her, but before her refusal, the child remarked: "My Papa Mirito said that you would buy everything for me, costly or cheap!"

Father Casimir's intention, no doubt, was not to coddle the child, but to alleviate in some way his orphanhood, that he might not feel the lack of his father. Nevertheless, when Louis was about three years old, he surprised Ramoncita by huddling in a corner, sad, thoughtful. With that attitude so unusual in a child, especially in one so vivacious, happy and playful, Ramoncita feared that he might be ill.

"What is the matter, Louis? Why are you sad? Are you sick?"

Louis shook his head, but he could hide nothing from his mother. Looking at her with that penetrating look of his, he said to her with a precocious seriousness: "I am thinking that my Papa Mirito is not my real papa."

The scenes that we contemplate in the first years of our life have a decisive influence upon our manner of being. Archbishop Martínez had the soul of an artist and all his life he was an admirer of the country. From childhood his bright eyes never tired contemplating the rural landscape to be seen on all sides; corn fields that stretched out until lost to sight; wheat fields ripened by the summer sun, with spikes swaying in the wind like a sea of gold, the Lerma River ever flowing, like life, among the fronds of age-old plants, and the whole landscape covered with the blue curvature of a clear sky. Later on, he would recall these first impressions.

There was a time when I beheld running under my feet a teeming river. It came from afar; in its long course it had received the torrent of its tributaries many times and, enriched with the treasure of many regions, impetuously rushed over the precipice, its crystalline waters crowned with foam and modulating a mysterious lullaby that seemed a lament, a sigh, the expression of deep, gigantic desire.[1]

In my youthful years, eager for inspiration and serenity, I used to enjoy climbing to the mountain tops, or burying myself in the bosom of shady forests, steeped in mystery. How often, reclining on an emerald hillside, looking at the crystal water shining like a silver thread in the bottom of the ravine, breathing in the fragrance of the simple wild flowers, I felt in my soul the gigantic symphony of that magnificent, untamed nature! It was indescribable and inimitable. One would say that all sounds had been blended into one mighty harmony. There was the screech of the wind on the tops of the lofty pines, the creaking of the tree trunks and the mysterious murmur of water running into the ravines. There was the rhythmic echo of the distant strokes of the ax, the sonorous and jubilant song, the drowsy buzzing of insects, the mysterious noise of the dead leaves as wary reptiles crawled over them; there were other multiple and varied sounds of whose origin I am ignorant, whose name I do not know, but which I feel in my soul in the magic sensibility of those sweet hours.

No dissonance in that magnificent hymn; no contrast broke the unity of that symphony as simple as majestic. Is there some genius who can enclose in one phrase all that nature says when it sings?[2]

But if mere things leave their indelible traces upon us, with greater reason is this true of the persons with whom we live. What was the influence of the observation of a country priest's arduous labor, day after day, hidden, full of abnegation, patience and charity? It is the secret of the influence that souls exert upon one another.

[1] Lecture at the Seminary of Morelia, September 27, 1922.
[2] Discourse at the silver episcopal anniversary of Bishop Leopoldo Ruiz, Morelia, 1925.

Louis, who had neither brothers and sisters nor friends with whom to play, used to imitate his "Papa Mirito," and, with a broom-stick for a horse, he would ride from one end of the patio to the other, to hear in all seriousness the confession of . . . a rose-bush! Again, mounted on a chair which served as a pulpit, he preached to the maids and if they did not pay attention, he reprimanded them with the force and vehemence that years later his word would have in the pulpit.

Some years later it was necessary to leave Molinos de Caballero, for Father Casimir had been assigned to the parish of Puruándiro. It was a definitive farewell, and when Louis, as Archbishop Martínez, passed through Molinos de Caballero, the enthusiasm of his countrymen was as great as his own emotion upon contemplating again those places filled with memories of his childhood. But everything passes in this world; and a few years afterwards, modern agriculture and the introduction of electricity into that region necessitated the building of a huge dam. Soon the waters covered everything: the old settlement, the immense plains, the valleys and ravines. It is now the great dam of Tepuxtepec.

The pastorate of Father Casimir in Puruándiro lasted but a few months; death claimed him at the height of his activity, on October 25, 1888. Louis, who was now seven years of age, realized perfectly his new orphanhood. He would never see "Papa Mirito" again, but the affection and gratitude for the one who was his second father would never be extinguished. Even as late as 1955 the Archbishop offered Mass for him on March 4 and, as in previous years, arranged for others as well.

When Ramoncita had fulfilled the final duties to her brother, she took her son and moved to Morelia, to seek the help of another brother, Sabino Rodríguez. He was a man of solid character, thoroughly honest, just, with an excellent practical judgment. His education was very limited because he had always worked in the country. He was the manager successively of two or three haciendas in the environs of Morelia.

Without ostentation, self-denyingly, with the hard work of the field, he financed the entire education of Louis and contributed in great measure to the formation of his nephew's character. He had the immense satisfaction of seeing him a priest and of assisting at his first Mass. Assisted in last illness by Father Martínez, he died in May, 1915.

Concerned about the education of her son, Ramoncita managed that he could devote himself to study from a very early age, first in Molinos de Caballero, afterwards in Puruándiro and finally in Morelia, where he finished his primary instruction.[3] In January, 1891, a boy, scarcely nine and a half years of age, knocked at the doors of the seminary in Morelia. He was the future Archbishop Primate of Mexico. His career there was most brilliant, and in all situations he maintained his place at the head of his companions. Two endowments were prominent in him: a phenomenal memory and an exceedingly keen intellect.

The boy who loses his father at a tender age can grow into adolescence with a certain lack of manliness, and more so if he is an only son. He usually becomes a spoiled child, capricious, to whom nothing may be refused, one who cannot be opposed in any way. Along this path it is impossible to acquire a manly disposition.

But the personality of Louis Martínez was characterized by a marked virility; he was a man in the entire acceptation of the

[3] Let us be more precise about the dates. The Archbishop lived in Molinos de Caballero from 1881 to 1886; in Morelia from the middle of 1886 to the beginning of 1887; in Puruándiro, from 1887 to the end of 1888; in Morelia from November, 1888, until April, 1937, except the period from December 1922 to September, 1923, during which he was Apostolic Administrator in Chilapa; in Mexico, from April, 1937, until his death, February 9, 1956.

word. How is this to be explained? Doubtless because Ramoncita was a copy of "the valiant woman" of Sacred Scripture. In
her were united two seemingly opposite qualities: an exquisite
tenderness and a spirited disposition.

She loved her son with an extraordinary love; but, like all
deep affections, it was divined rather than manifested exteriorly.
Reserved with words of endearment and caresses, she did not
excuse herself from any sacrifice for her son. And how well
Louis learned and practiced that lesson of abnegation and sacrifice! Nothing is so capable of strengthening the will as sacrifice
and renunciation.

His uncle, Sabino Rodríguez, also contributed to the formation of his character. Life in the country is austere, laborious
and a forger of "men." There Sabino was formed and his example influenced the formation of the young seminarian. At
that time, Louis was spending the vacation periods with his
uncle, on the hacienda of which he was manager. Consequently,
he became a consummate horseman. His uncle had given him a
horse for his exclusive use, and he named it "Birdie." The animal was a thoroughbred; to manage it, neither spur nor whip
was necessary, the bridle rein sufficed. A movement of the reins
and the horse seemed to sense the will of its master, now to dart
forth like an arrow, now to leap over obstacles, now to stop on
the instant, now to cut capers like a spirited charger.

During the seminary vacations, Louis frequently saddled
Birdie, took his rifle and, accompanied by his dog, "Indian," set
out to hunt. When the prey—ducks, quails— was within shoot-
ing range he stopped the horse, dropped the bridle rein, took
aim, and fired. Birdie remained motionless as a statue, in spite
of the detonation. On the other hand, Indian ran to pick up the
fallen prey, and holding it in his mouth, stood with forepaws
upon the horse, to present it to his master. The hunter took the
booty, put it into his saddle-bags, and continued onward.

From early childhood, Louis Martínez began to ride a horse,

and unlike other children who needed a servant to hold them in the saddle and another to carry the reins, he supported himself alone, and all alone he guided the animal. On one occasion an excited horse ran away with him, crossing plains, climbing hills. The danger was very great, for at any moment, the child could fall off, be dragged or kicked by the horse, or the animal could plunge into the brambles and crags, which would be equally disastrous. Nothing could be done. To run after the horse would be to frighten him the more. The powerless witnesses looked on at the spectacle with an anguish that can be imagined.

But Louis gave proof of remarkable nervous equilibrium; not for one moment did he lose his serenity or mastery of himself. Like a good horseman, he held the reins firmly and maintained his balance in the saddle. The horse finally arrived at a village where the streets themselves formed a corral. Panting and perspiring, the horse stopped his mad race and Louis dismounted triumphantly.

The discipline and the life of piety in the seminary also played a part in the formation of Louis' character, and Monsignor Banegas, who died as Bishop of Querétaro, had a decisive influence on this formation. Too little known and appreciated, he was a man ahead of his time, of broad vision, accurate judgment, and an insight that bordered almost on prophecy.

When the religious conflict was settled in 1929, there was a certain wonderment among some Catholics who asked: "How can the Church yield any of her rights?" Monsignor Banegas had found the solution some time before.

"The Church," he said, "has two classes of rights; some primary and fundamental, which cannot be yielded; others, secondary, which can be yielded to avoid greater evils, especially temporarily, until those critical circumstances pass away." Therefore, he was of the opinion that a fitting arrangement could be made so that worship would not be suspended in

1926, and that, sooner or later, things would return to their normal state. But the situation was so hostile, so confused, minds so excited, opinions so inclined to resistance that it was not possible to follow his opinion. Time and events, nevertheless, have shown that he was right.

Long before the religious persecution was even conjectured, Monsignor Banegas had a presentiment of it. In 1912 he gathered together all the seminary professors and told them that he foresaw sad days for the Church and especially for the seminary; that they would not be able to support either the seminarians or the professors.

"I wish to know," he said seriously, and weighing his words, "whom among you I can count upon to continue teaching gratuitously, when such a time arrives." All gave their word to remain at their post in spite of everything. Two years later that day came; in 1914, the seminary was robbed of its building and of its means of subsistence. For years, not one cent could be given to the professors; but all fulfilled their pledge.

Archbishop Martínez was the masterpiece of Bishop Banegas. And neither the one nor the other failed to recognize it, for the more the latter kept it secret, the more the former proclaimed it to the four winds. When Louis Martínez was appointed bishop the first thing that he did was to inform Bishop Banegas, inviting him as assisting bishop and asking for his fatherly blessing. Bishop Banegas accepted the invitation, but he refused to give the blessing, since both were bishops.

Bishop Martínez insisted, appealing to the right of paternity which Bishop Banegas had upon him. He yielded at last and blessed him with the blessing of Jacob: "A growing son, and comely to behold" (Gen. 49:22).

Archbishop Martínez attended Bishop Banegas in his final sickness. In spite of being overwhelmed with work, he found time to make trips to Querétaro to visit him in his long, painful illness (pulmonary cancer) and to assist him in his last hour.

When Archbishop Martínez was named a member of the Language Academy, he first thought of composing his reception discourse upon the beauty of the Spanish language. But afterward he changed his mind and dedicated his discourse to Bishop Banegas. With that speech, the last that he wrote, he fulfilled a sacred duty of gratitude.

Such were the instruments of which God availed himself to forge the character of Archbishop Martínez and to make of him a complete man.

In 1891, as we have seen, Louis Martínez began his preparatory studies. In 1897 he entered the major seminary to study sacred theology. Among his professors was the Very Rev. Joaquín Sáenz Arciga, who was also his spiritual director for many years. On March 26, 1901, Louis Martínez received the clerical tonsure from the hands of Archbishop Silva. As he was only twenty years of age, it was necessary to wait at least three years to receive the priestly ordination.

In Morelia there was no center of higher learning other than the seminary, since the College of St. Nicholas had been converted into a secular, anticlerical center. Hence, not only those who aspired to the priesthood, but Catholic youths desiring to follow other careers as well, entered the minor seminary. In order to remedy the disadvantages which this arrangement entailed, the Archbishop of Michoacán founded the Institute of the Sacred Heart, where young men who did not feel called to the priesthood could follow the preparatory course. Father Joseph López Ortega was named rector, Rev. Mr. John B. Buitrón, vice-rector, and Rev. Mr. Louis M. Martínez, prefect of discipline. These last two were not yet priests.

In his free time Reverend Mr. Martínez devoted himself to study and to reading. During that period, he aimed to read and to assimilate all the works of Lacordaire. This accounts for Lacordaire's influence upon his oratorical flights in later years. From time to time he even quoted Lacordaire literally.

About twenty-five years afterwards, in reading the biography of Dom Guéranger, written by Dom Delatte, he found some aspersions cast upon Lacordaire. In a letter to a friend of his, Bishop Martínez wrote:

I have just finished reading the biography of Dom Guéranger. What a man! Perhaps the first, or at least, among the first, of France in his age.

I am enchanted with the book and disenchanted with men. I certainly have had enough experience with humankind not to be appalled by their miseries, but it is very painful to see men who have been loved and who have exerted a powerful influence in our life, like Lacordaire and Dupanloup, fall from their pedestal. The biography of a man is irremediably disillusioning when that man is not a saint.

And then comes the sally of good humor: "Everyone not trying to be a saint is going to the dogs!"[4]

On June 9, 1904, Louis Martínez reached his twenty-third birthday, and now, with an indult from the Holy See, he could be ordained priest. Archbishop Silva conferred the priesthood upon him on November 20 in the chapel of the archbishop's palace. We might note here that the Church celebrated that

---

[4] At first, Dom Guéranger, Abbot of Solesmes, and Lacordaire, restorer of the Dominicans in France, were united by sincere friendship, thanks to the mediation of Mme. Swetchine. Lacordaire gave Dom Guéranger the first confidence about his vocation, and the counsel and the example of the Abbot of Solesmes encouraged him and sustained him in restoring the Dominican Order in France. In June, 1838, before leaving for Rome to make his novitiate, Lacordaire made a retreat in Solesmes, under the direction of Dom Guéranger and in the latter's cell that matter which brought such great good to the Church and to souls was settled.

But Dom Guéranger and Lacordaire were not souls that could understand each other for a long time; different in education, formation and tendencies, the very movement of life had to carry them in divergent directions. The liberalistic tendencies of Lacordaire eventually brought about a conflict with the Abbot of Solesmes, whose absolute fidelity to the Holy See was the rule of his life.

As for Msgr. Dupanloup, he was one of the most tenacious objectors in the Vatican Council to the declaration of the infallibility of the Pope.

year the golden jubilee of the dogmatic definition of the Immaculate Conception. Morelia observed it with extraordinary splendor, for in October the First National Marian Congress was held there.

According to the custom in the archdiocese of Michoacán, the new priest did not celebrate any Mass before his first solemn Mass. This first Mass was on Christmas Day in Holy Cross Church in Morelia. Father Martínez waited so many days before offering his first Mass because the feast of Christmas was always for him something exceptional. Thirty-eight years afterwards he wrote in his private notes:

What a Christmas I spent! Decidedly this is my own feast. I never fail to weep on that night and I never fail to be affected. Not even in my most distracted hours did I cease experiencing the heavenly emotion of that night.

On the Christmas that has just passed, the impression upon my soul was very calm, very deep and very sweet. How can I possibly explain it? Ever since, my peace has a seal of security, as if neither Jesus nor I could doubt our mutual love.

A few days before, for some unknown reason, the doubt came to me whether my heart belonged to Jesus completely and solely; and this doubt made my heart react in such a way, as if hurt, as if it protested against the suspicion, that in one impetuous, supreme impulse it surrendered to Jesus so that it could no longer doubt but that it is all his.

Now then, this contributed perhaps to the security of that night; I possessed the Child in my soul with the peace of true possession, with the certainty that not anyone nor anything could tear my precious treasure away from me. And he himself so possessed me, binding the two of us in such a way that we were each for the other in the full security of our mutual love.

How I relish the Introit of the third Mass (his high Mass): "A Child is born to us and a son is given to us whose empire is upon his shoulders." And in that charming Child is the mystery, the sublimity, the marvel, the fullness of the divinity!

The first Mass was exceedingly tender, with emotion, with tears. The *"Adeste fideles"* and other Christmas hymns penetrated my soul like sharp, yet gentle, darts. After the Consecration, I could scarcely stand up under the presence of Jesus in the Sacred Host. . . . And the rest of the Masses, tranquil, gentle, with the peace and calm of possession.

During the adoration at the Crib, after the Mass, they sang a very touching Christmas hymn: *"Duerme, no llores,"* and I can never hear it on that lovely Night without weeping.

It may be asked how His Excellency managed to hide his tears, for no one ever saw him weep. Could it be that his tears were those that only the heart weeps?

We shall understand the importance that Christmas held for the Archbishop when we realize that his spirituality had a notable tinge of "spiritual infancy." Perhaps also, for the same reason, he almost always selected this season of the year to make his annual retreat.

During the new scholastic year of 1905 the entire personnel of the Institute was changed and Father Martínez was named prefect of discipline at the seminary. Archbishop Silva continued working in his seminary and he dreamed of placing it at the top of the best of its kind. To do this, he needed the right man; he found him in Canon Banegas, at that time secretary to the Archbishop. He was named rector in 1906 and launched upon an arduous, difficult task: to restore discipline, to promote a solid piety and to change completely the program of studies and the methods of teaching.

In his turn, Canon Banegas sought a co-worker who would enter fully into his views. He found him in the recently ordained priest, Father Martínez, who was named vice-rector, an office which lasted until 1919, when he was officially appointed rector. In fact he had been so since 1913, when the Holy See entrusted to Canon Banegas the government of the diocese of Vera Cruz as Apostolic Administrator.

The secret of success when one undertakes an enterprise is to find the right man, the right man in the right place. This was the talent of Archbishop Silva, who discovered Canon Banegas; and of Canon Banegas, who selected Father Martínez as his vice-rector.

Canon Banegas was the mind that directed, but Father Martínez was the will that put into execution the preconceived ideal. Canon Banegas marked out the course; Father Martínez directed the operation. He rode the tempests that agitated the ship of the seminary and were at the point of submerging it, until he brought it into quiet waters. The impression that Archbishop Martínez left upon the seminary during the thirty-two years of his government can never be erased.

In the matter of discipline, there became established, not a military discipline by fear and force, but an almost monastic discipline, through conviction and supernatural viewpoints. The seminary functioned with the precision of a clock and the regularity of a cloister.

An example is illustrative of this point. On one occasion Father Martínez wanted to find out if the order was the result of fear of punishment or if it was observed through conviction. So he announced to the whole college that, on the following day, all the prefects would have a holiday and that the students need obey only their own conscience and the bell. Never was there better order and regularity than on that day.

In the matter of piety, frequentation of the sacraments, mental prayer, spiritual conferences, retreats and the exercises were prudently promoted. In the program of studies, the system of progressive cycles was established so that each subject was seen in its entirety each year, but each time with greater amplitude. Great importance was given to the natural sciences such as physics, chemistry, geology, minerology, biology. And just as Monsignor Abarca had introduced Scholastic philosophy in 1884, Father Martínez introduced Neo-Scholasticism, following the way marked out by the future Cardinal Mercier, in the University of Louvain. All of this contributed to place the theological studies at a high level.

At this period, Father Martínez specialized in philosophical studies. He studied the works of St. Thomas, and among his commentators his favorite was Cajetan. We often saw him deeply engaged in those voluminous parchments in the library, or studying the philosophical works of the University of Louvain, or modern treatises on biology, especially on what relates to the functioning of the brain and of the nervous system, which holds such great importance in the study of psychology.

As a completion of his philosophical formation, he held the chair of philosophy several years, he published a textbook for the first cycle and annotations for the second. His classes were a delight; the two hours daily that he employed in teaching seemed but a moment to his students. Never did he use a text book, notes or any other guide. He used to walk while he talked. His exposition was so clear, so luminous, that no place was left for doubts. We were all hanging on his lips and it never occurred to anyone to be inattentive or to play a prank.

Two incidents show that he was a recognized philosopher: he merited special praise from the University of Louvain and he was elected to take part in the Congress of Scientists in Mexico in 1912, attended by the most distinguished intellectuals in the country. Before this assembly he read a study of Positivist philosophy, which was praised highly in spite of the fact that it encountered different, even opposing, mentalities.

His philosophical studies carried to such a depth were truly providential, for upon the vigorous training of his intellect, God planted the solid foundation for studies as difficult as dangerous—those of mysticism, both speculative and practical, to which, years later, he would have to devote himself in the direction of souls and in his own interior life.

The seminary had reached its peak when the storm broke.

Carranza's forces were preparing to make their entry into Morelia; the alarm spread through the city. The superiors, as a measure of prudence, resolved to evacuate the seminary. The boarding students were given over to their guardians, the clergy were distributed among Christian families.

It was the night of July 31, 1914. At a very late hour the evacuation of the building was completed. There remained only the vice-rector, Father Martínez, and two or three Fathers who left at dawn.

How I remember, as if it were yesterday, that final night! We were walking with the vice-rector through the solitary cloisters, bathed in moonlight, without making up our minds to leave these walls that enclosed a tradition of a century. Our hearts were wrung with the presentiment that this would be a definitive farewell.

We will understand this better, as well as how Archbishop Martínez had identified his life with the seminary, from his own words at a dinner which the seminary tendered to Bishop Banegas, then bishop of Querétaro, on the night of June 27, 1927.

The immortal remembrance lives in my spirit. To the sweet melancholy of an awards program there was united that afternoon the sadness of a farewell and the bitterness of a presentiment. We knew that you were going to leave, Your Excellency, and we sensed that your absence would be very long, definitive perhaps. We said nothing, but there floated in the atmosphere what the lips refused to formulate. Surrounding us was that air of indefinable anguish, which the Latin poet described in those immortal lines: *Sunt lacrimae rerum et corda mortalia tangunt.*

We saw you depart; and afterwards came the solemn, tragic, indescribable catastrophe. We saw the past ruined, our past, the one we had lovingly formed with our sweat, our tears, the one that rose at the magic conjuration of your voice, illuminated with the splendid light of Christ, welded with the fire of our noble desires.

Just as the farmer sees the fertile field devastated by the storm, as the father of the family contemplates the home crumbling away, as Jesus gazed with tear-filled eyes upon the gigantic ruin of his own country, so we heard first the old manorial house crackle under the onrush of savage profanations; and afterwards we saw it swaying, and at last converted into a heap of desolate ruins.

We lost everything, Your Excellency, even the right to live; and wrapped in the mantle of desperation I might have uttered the heart-rending lamentations of the prophet over those sacred, beloved ruins, if my eyes had not been turned toward heaven, if my heart had not been established so powerfully in hope.

But it pleased God that we might save from the terrible cataclysm what was dearest and most precious: the old vellum of our forefathers, the beautiful coat of arms with its unstained heraldry.

Lovingly we preserved the treasure and we have even augmented it; we placed on the legendary shield a new emblem; it is an iron cross spattered with blood.

Today we see you again, no longer in the rich, comfortable house of our forefathers but in this very poor, yet glorious corner, glorious because the heroic figures of Portugal and of Munguía are erected in it and because here our life arises, like an immortal hope. Today we see you again removed from us by the loftiness of your dignity, but very near also because our affections have been refined. I wish to tell you, Your Excellency, that I keep unharmed the treasure you entrusted to my unretracted loyalty upon your departure. You will not find the house of our forefathers that was desecrated, nor the ancient wealth that was destroyed, nor your many co-workers who died or emigrated; but you will find the same order, the same studies, the same spirit; you will find that with loving respect we have guarded, as a priceless treasure, your work.

All this is signified by this simple, intimate, affectionate celebration that we proffer you with all the sincerity of our heart; what it expresses with irresistible eloquence can be condensed into this sentence:

Your Excellency, everything has been lost, everything; except the greatness of your work and the immensity of our love!

CHAPTER II

Maturity

THE NATURAL CHARACTER of Archbishop Martínez was of a manifestly virile type, as we have already noted. That trait was responsible for a reserve in demonstrations of feeling. In the early years of his priesthood he appeared, at first view, as an insensitive man, devoid of heart. It was just the contrary, as we shall see later. It takes courage to restrain our feelings, to forbid ourselves manifestations of fondness. While these outward expressions are satisfying to ourselves, they may foster egoism. Only that love is genuine which proves itself by sacrifice.

Let us give some evidences of the Archbishop's austerity. It is a point of importance because it shows us how far he was from over-sentimentality and because it helps us to evaluate his spirituality.

Few have had so full a communication of spiritual paternity as Archbishop Martínez, a gift he received in a special manner when he was consecrated bishop. According to his teaching, the episcopate is the sacrament of the Father, as the priesthood is the sacrament of the Son, and the diaconate, of the Holy Spirit. And the distinguishing characteristic of the Father is fecundity.

His spiritual paternity reached its zenith in 1927. On September 21 of that year he received a remarkable grace of spiritual fruitfulness. In his private notes we find these words to our Lord:

"On Good Friday you said some things to me. . . . O Jesus, is it possible that my poor love takes that aspect which humbles me, that you keep expanding in my soul that new, vehement

19

desire of paternity? What a mystery of love and of suffering began to unfold before my eyes!"

Therefore, the heart of the Archbishop, filled with charity, reflected the paternity of God. He had a keen consciousness of being a father of souls, especially of those whom God had entrusted to him in a special manner. He had then the right, and he could take justifiable satisfaction in calling by the dear name of children those who were really so spiritually. Nevertheless, he never did so.

He did, of course, place in his Pastorals the customary salutation: "Venerable Brethren and well beloved children," but it was only as a phrase proper to the Curia. In his sermons and in his letters I have not found this expression one single time. We who received spiritually from him often would have liked to hear him call us by the endearing name of sons. Never did he give us that pleasure nor did he take it for himself. He thus fulfilled the resolution he had made: "Not to relish legitimate and due pleasures."

The Archbishop comprehended the sacerdotal and the episcopal paternity with deepest appreciation. He wrote in his personal notes:

There is a love that looks for the Beloved everywhere and finds him everywhere. To such a lover the words of St. Paul are clear and luminous: "In him all things hold together" (Col. 3:11).

But there is another love that does not seek the Beloved, but which carries him everywhere and reproduces him unceasingly. One can scarcely speak of this mystery. Such is priestly love, which accomplishes at the altar the Eucharistic prodigy. In holy Mass we can repeat, as an audacious echo, the words of the Father: "Thou art my Son: this day I have begotten thee" (Ps. 2:7).

Such is priestly love, which enkindles in the darkness of sinful souls the unfailing light of Christ. Such is priestly love, which slowly and patiently keeps carving in souls Jesus' adorable features.

The mission of the priest is to form Jesus, to cause him to be born and to grow up, as the holy Child grew in age, wisdom and grace; to make him develop in souls until they reach the fullness of the age of Christ.

The pastoral solicitude of the bishop tends to form Jesus, not only in souls, but, we might say, in the Church, which has been entrusted to him.

The essential role of history is the reproduction of Jesus in souls, in people, in the whole extent of the earth.

My mission is to produce and to develop Jesus everywhere in a mysterious way. What happiness, what glory! And the graces of 1927 give to my love an especial fecundity. The apostolic life appears to my mind in a new form. A priest, an apostle, is a man who has for his mission the reproducing of Jesus everywhere. A new revelation, the apostolic life is love, fecund love, love that reproduces Jesus!

To reproduce Jesus in souls, to engender Jesus in them, is to be their spiritual father, and to have the entire right to call them children. He did not give himself, I repeat, that satisfaction.

We present another proof of his austerity and of the repugnance of his virile nature for excessive sentimentality. It is a clever letter in which one does not know which to admire the more, his fine irony, his delicacy in reprimanding without wounding, or the exquisite literary style. Here it is.

Dear friend:

I cannot resist the temptation to write to you my impressions of the Corpus Christi procession that I have just attended. I thought it a romantic scene. The tabernacle on the main altar was enclosed within a multi-colored cloud whose tints gave the softness of fantasy to the mysterious light enveloping it. Romantic also were the *posas*,[1] covered with gauze and populated with living angels dressed in silk. I saw a dove floating over them in a ruddy light and flaming

---

[1] Small altars where the Blessed Sacrament was placed during a pause in processions.

hearts with mystical legends which I did not succeed in deciphering, and Peace and Purity frisking upon the voluptuous softness of skies at dawn.

But the dominant note of the solemnity was, beyond a doubt, the fair choir of virgins who, carrying the symbolic lamps in their hands and embalming the atmosphere with the perfume distilled from their fingers, glided gently along before the tabernacle, like that mysterious Ophelia, who in a tragic scene in Hamlet, passes by scattering flowers and singing.

Certainly, some of the fair virgins seemed so uneasy that my spirit's scant devotion was disturbed, fearing that the oil in their lamps might be lacking when the wedding party would arrive. They swayed constantly! They sang so loudly, so dramatically! They ascended the altar steps with such assurance, even elbowing the sacred ministers!

When the procession ended, my colloquy, or rather, my interior soliloquy might have been expressed in these terms: No doubt, it is human to put a touch of sensuous poetry into the sacred ceremonies, but to impregnate the liturgy with romanticism, will this not prejudice its spiritual and solemn gravity? Or rather, is it that the manly, austere school in which I was educated hinders my spirit from adapting itself to other esthetic forms? You, with your mystical, artistic bent and your strong Benedictine inclinations, can judge the matter. If you succeed in solving the problem, communicate the solution to your devoted friend,

Louis M. Martínez.[2]

But we would be greatly mistaken if we judged the Archbishop to be a person of slight feelings. The contrary is the case. That austerity was only the rind that partly hid and partly protected a delicate sensitiveness which we might even classify as hypersensitiveness. But he knew well how to dissimulate it. Only the very few who penetrated into the interior of his soul realized that his whole being responded to kindness, beauty,

[2] Letter to J. G. T., June 3, 1926.

and harmony. His soul was moved by gratitude and friendship, as well as by the sorrows and sufferings of others.

He was a votary of friendship of the style of Lacordaire. None of his friends could complain that he betrayed their friendship, despite the fact that his life was a constant ascent until he reached the highest place in the ecclesiastical hierarchy of Mexico, while some of them remained at ground level. He never changed; he was always the same.

His friendship was marked by two conspicuous qualities: fidelity and delicacy. Despite the fact that he was a staunch friend of gentleness, he was very candid; still, one sensed his delicacy. If it was his duty to reprimand a friend, he did it without human respect or culpable weakness, but with fine tact so as not to hurt. He even spoke as if he were apologizing for what had only been his duty.

For example, he said to a very sensitive person: "You are too touchy; I am like the maguey." To another impetuous character: "You seem like a bull ready for the arena. I am like a tame ox; no matter how much they prod him with the pike, he doesn't hasten his pace." The reality was very different.

This selection from a letter shows us the same trait:

Your next to the last letter brought me pain and admiration: pain, for having bothered you so much when you were bilious; and admiration that the bile was poured out on you and not on me. The commentary I made was to repeat pathetically that familiar expression of Father López Ortega:[3] "Alas, unhappy the man born sensitive!"

I confess to you that *in illo tempore* the profundity of the remark did not penetrate me and I supposed it a ready-made phrase taken from some romantic, tearful song or from an ordinary

[3] Father José López Ortega was professor of philosophy in the seminary of Morelia and afterwards rector of the Scientific Institute of the Sacred Heart of Jesus; he was a very distinguished scholarly priest. He died prematurely.

comedy.[4] We simple mortals have little to suffer and we diminish
that little by letting it glide by gently, . . . but *you* with that spiritual hyperaesthesia! You eventually have to pay for the divine
hyperaesthesia of art with the hyperaesthesia of bilious reactions.
O most wise Father López Ortega, how right you were!

Again, his sensitiveness was betrayed in his filial affection;
how he loved his mother! When in the midst of his absorbing
occupations as vice-rector he succeeded in escaping to see her,
few things were said with his lips, but how many with his look!

Love is said to be intuitive, especially when it is pure and
ardent. Why was there need of words for those two hearts that
through the intuitions of love understood and interpreted each
other? Well might he include in his personal notes this reference to divine love:

"What is a look of love? Is it love that goes forth from the
eyes or is it the soul seeking in the beloved the sweet incentive
to love? Is love's glance surrender or possession? When one
looks, does he express love or ask for it? Oh, who can explain
the mystery of a look of love?"

When Bishop Martínez' mother died on February 9, 1925, a
wound was opened in his heart never to be healed. Years later
he wrote in his diary: "The wound opened in my soul by my
mother's death has not been closed; perhaps it will not be closed
in this world. Today I retraced places filled with memories of
her; my heart was moved and tears sprang to my eyes."

But then comes the generosity of divine love to master
everything:

I said to God: If to evoke the sweet remembrance of my mother
and to relish it is contrary to your love, I will sacrifice to you even
that recollection, for I want to sacrifice all for you, for you are my
only One; she taught me to love you above all things. Then a
swift, soft light flooded my soul, like the answer of God to my
words.

[4] The expression in reality is taken from a poem by Núñez de Arce.

Then I began to comprehend what divinized affections are, that is, the affections of heaven are initiated on earth with the imperfections of exile. Souls are united through thought and love. Could there be greater union than that which has for its bond the divine thought and the will of God? The blessed in heaven and holy souls on earth have simplified their thoughts and affections in the single thought and simple love of God.

This is the true unity of souls and, consequently, the true love. How different are those divinized affections from human affections! The latter are poor and petty because they never attain perfect unity. The true affections that the heart longs for are reflections and prolongations of the only Love. Two souls who love each other are deified souls, submerged in the love of God. What purity in those affections that dwell in the bosom of God! What disinterestedness, what intimacy, what sweetness, what liberty!

Thus they love in heaven, the true fatherland of love. Thus we can love on earth. Certainly here those holy affections have the imperfection attendant upon exile; but even so, how much better they are than mere human fondness!

The foundation of those holy affections is faith; and faith is always obscure. That sensible contact so sought for by our wretchedness is lacking to those souls that love one another in this way but are separated by death or distance; but in the midst of the shades of faith, they find one another, they communicate with one another, and they are united in God.

In heaven, that animated fellowship will not be lacking to souls that love another; at first, divinely spiritual; after the resurrection, marvelously sensible.

On earth the darkness of faith is a deficiency, but it is also a safeguard. Are not sensible communications here below an obstacle to purity, to disinterestedness, to the intimacy of the affections? Are they not a source of egoism? Are they not a weight that takes away from souls the freedom to unite and ascend?

The true love, the only love, is the divine; the others, if they are true, are irradiations from it. As in the daytime the only light is the light of the sun and this can come to us directly from its own center or be reflected upon objects, taking diverse colors and shades or screened in transparent mediums, dressed with the rich colors of the rainbow, so in the world of souls, God is the only sun of love; all affections are light from that sun reflected or screened in creatures or which floods purified eyes with divinest splendor.

Love always has something of the divine, something of the immense; to appreciate its truth and to define its degrees, one must appreciate the divine within it. What a pity that words are forced in vain to translate what the divine light expresses without words!

Since these pages were not written for anyone else, they reveal to us how the great heart of Archbishop Martínez loved.

Another evidence of the Archbishop's refined sensibility was his artistic temperament. Not only is that person an artist who creates beauty, but also he who is capable of admiring it. Either to produce a work of art or to understand it, one needs an esthetic sense. Without an artistic temperament, how can one adequately appreciate beauty?

It suffices to read some pages written by the Archbishop to understand that he was an excellent litterateur. For example, who can make a literary description out of the high sea, if he sees only water, and more water? In his book, *A Propósito De Un Viaje* the Archbishop wrote an entire chapter upon the ocean. Let us select some lines:

During these days I have seen much of the sea and I have seen it with love. Its beauty lies in its great simplicity. All grandeur, all sublimity are characterized by simplicity. Below lies the complicated, the complex; above, on the summit, dwells the simple.

Some may think that the ocean is monotonous; but it is not so. It is rich in color, in line; nevertheless, none of these things constitutes its beauty. Its grandeur, its power to attract, to captivate, to fascinate lie in its immensity.

Sky and ocean speak to us of the infinite better than anything else; the sky is the immensity that is embraced neither with the eyes nor the imagination; this poor faculty of ours experiences a dizziness when it wants to dream of immense space. The ocean is the relative immensity; although we may not see its shores, we know its limits; it is nearer us; it is the immensity that expands under our feet; the palpable immensity, our own immensity.

Sometimes the ocean overwhelms us with its vast expanse and sometimes we feel it our brother; sometimes it seems to smile upon us with its splendid placidity, with the gentle vibration of its waves, with the soft colors that tint its crystal; still smiling, it makes us feel our indisputable smallness. But sometimes it becomes magnificent, terrible. I have not seen a storm at sea, but I have seen them in souls; they are terribly beautiful. The tempests on the ocean must be like them.

The ocean is not monotonous; in the simplicity of its beauty is hidden the gamut of color and of sound, the variety of line and of form, and especially, a hidden richness that no language can express, but which the spirit feels, as if in the capricious lines of its waves, in the immaculate whiteness of its foam, in the shades of its colors and in the mystery of its horizons, the ocean were hiding something spiritual and divine that communicates itself to our spirit, revealing secrets that lips may not tell.

If God put something divine in all creatures, the imprint of his hand, the breath of his Spirit, the fragrance of his majesty, it seems that the divine in the ocean is discovered more easily to the spirit; because the multiple, petty things of earth do not disturb it, or because the ineffable solitude of the ocean disposes the spirit to perceive God the better.

Here is another page written by the Archbishop:

Precious the destiny of flowers: to diffuse their fragrance toward heaven and to deposit their fecund seed in the earth.

What does it matter that their springtime is ephemeral and their freshness fleeting, that the luxuriance of their petals is scattered like a rapid dream, if their aroma has imbued the atmosphere, if their immortal germ will never be lost?

Souls are like flowers: beneath the wealth of their virtues or under the wrapping of their wretchedness they hide a heavenly fragrance and a prolific seed. Their perfume is love, their virginal fruit is Jesus, whom, in one form or other, they communicate to other souls.

Upon becoming flesh, the Word of God was changed into the divine Gardener; enamored of souls, he sows untiringly the seed from heaven, he breathes with gratification the exquisite fragrance of their flowers and he lovingly gathers the rich harvest.

What do those souls have that Jesus loves them like that? What can that divine perfume be that they guard within so mysteriously? Who can understand that divine something that the Creator lavished upon them with his omnipotent breath, that Jesus watered with his blood, that the Holy Spirit fertilized with his sanctifying shadow?

Perhaps the springtime of souls is also fleeting, passing with its unforgettable charms, its immaculate freshness, it celestial dreams, but what does it matter, if souls, like flowers, fulfill their blessed destiny when they reach their autumnal maturity; if they diffuse toward heaven their divine fragrance and deposit upon other souls their immortal seed?

Archbishop Martínez was an artist not only in prose, but also in verse; but his modesty about his poems was such that they were unknown during his life-time, except some humorous verses. On the contrary, he made jests about poets, saying that our Lord, who did all things well, had never composed verses.

When in the year 1933 he visited Niagara Falls, that stupendous spectacle reminded him of the intimate story of his own spiritual life, the vicissitudes through which he had passed, his struggles, his trials, even the happy day upon which the "hour of love" sounded, when his soul, transfigured in Christ, received the ineffable caresses of divine love. Then, in a magnificent poem, "Niagara Falls," he sang his own story of love with genuine mystic inspiration. To understand these verses and penetrate their profound meaning, we would need the commentary of the author himself.[5]

[5] Examples of his poetry can be found in the Spanish edition of this biography (Trans.).

Archbishop Martínez held a theory about artists, original, no doubt, but one that cannot be denied if it is seriously considered. According to His Excellency, nobody is an artist in just one field, in one manifestation of art, without being so in all lines. He will not always be an active artist, but he will at least be passive; he will not create beauty, but he will know how to admire it.

Perhaps the basic reason for this statement lies in the fact that beauty is fundamentally one single entity. God is the only, the absolute beauty; all beauty in the universe neither is nor can be anything else than a reflection of that supreme beauty.

Now, the Archbishop was a litterateur, therefore, he was an artist in all lines, that is to say, he was capable of enjoying all beauty, of finding delight in all loveliness. He was not properly a musician, but he listened to such music as Beethoven's *Ninth Symphony* with deep satisfaction. He possessed an unerring instinct for distinguishing religious music from so-called church music. Throughout his life he worked to restore religious music, especially Gregorian chant, first in the seminary, then in the Archdiocese of Morelia and afterwards in Mexico City. He did this not only in a spirit of submission to the directive of the Holy See, but also through his own personal taste. As for the plastic arts, he became enraptured upon contemplating the works of art in the Prado Museum in Madrid, in the Vatican Art Gallery, and in the Roman basilicas with their mosaics and frescoes. Beyond a doubt, Archbishop Martínez had an artistic temperament.

One more trait must be mentioned to complete our description of the character and the temperament of the Archbishop. That trait is his constant good humor, his serene equanimity, his unfailing optimism, his sane, contagious joy. He always had the opportune word, the inoffensive joy. He always had the witty anecdote. No one could be sad in his company.

In his maturity, that equanimity was, no doubt, the fruit of consummate virtue; but if we try to investigate its genesis, we shall find it in his remarkable nervous equilibrium. His physicians marvelled at this equilibrium and they attributed to it his untiring energy. He would spend long hours in study or in the works of the sacred ministry such as preaching, confirming and hearing confessions. When asked if he were tired, he would reply: "I do not have the poor taste to get tired." After many hours of fasting and working, he was once asked if he had a headache (a common ailment in such cases). He replied very very much in earnest: "But, how does the head ache?"

A certain prelate, realizing that he himself could not withstand so much work as the Archbishop, said to him: "I do not have a *glorified* body like Your Excellency!"

That same well balanced nervous system made him appear calm, unhurried, devoid of that overriding pressure and anxiety to undertake another work before the preceding task is finished. He applied himself to each task as if he had nothing else to do, in conformity with the maxim: *Age quod agis.*

One of the most troublesome occupations of a prelate is the spending of long hours daily receiving persons of all classes, some who come only to beg money, others who drag out their business tediously when they could tell it in a few words, others who do not listen to reason and who keep insisting on the very same things with a nerve-racking obstinacy.

Archbishop Martínez listened to each person as if he had to receive no one else. He had the rare gift of treating all in such a manner that none went away disgruntled although he might not have obtained his request.

From this same equilibrium proceeded his exceptional ability to sleep well. To lay his head on the pillow and to fall asleep were one. The serious, thorny problems attendant upon his responsibilities did not deprive him of sleep. "Last night," he used to say playfully, "I had a bad attack of insomnia; it took me two or three minutes to fall asleep."

In view of these varied circumstances, it is evident that His Excellency was always in good humor. He had great troubles, no doubt, and in his spiritual life terrible crises, as we shall see; but his humility, his confidence in God, his love for the divine will maintained him in peace, in spite of everything.

A short-sighted and narrow-minded observer once judged ill of Archbishop Martínez' humor, as if it detracted from the prelatial dignity or indicated levity and superficiality. What happened was that the Archbishop became "all things to all men to win all to Christ." He was wise with the wise, spiritual with the spiritual, a child with children, ignorant, as it were, with the ignorant, and with the frivolous society of our time he spoke, too, in the only language it can understand.

In this respect, as in other points, Archbishop Martínez closely resembled St. Francis de Sales. In the seventeenth century piety had become unsociable, prudish and seemingly incompatible with the healthy joy of living; St. Francis made it attractive, sweet, happy, and he was able, in this way to introduce it into the Court itself.

Archbishop Martínez did something similar. How many persons, estranged from God, prejudiced against priests and especially against the hierarchy, changed completely, rectifying their judgments before his conquering amiability and simplicity. On the other hand, the common people, the needy classes, were accustomed to see but few prelates, at a most respectful distance, never dealing with them directly but through a series of intermediaries. Consequently, they did not know the dignitaries. Such was the custom demanded by the times.

The Archbishop was a *democratic* prelate, in the good acceptation of the word. He placed himself directly in contact with his people, he knew their needs, he shared their sufferings and, so far as he could, he tried to remedy them. The result was that he gained the hearts of all. The extraordinary, universal grief at his death gave evidence of this fact.

Moreover, Archbishop Martínez was always himself—simple, natural, unpretentious, without studied attitudes, without poses. Sometimes in the ministry he even seemed distracted, as if he were lacking in devotion. Was it that he was trying to conceal the richness of his interior life? Or was he abstracted when he appeared distracted? I am more inclined to this latter opinion because he abhorred all pretense.

Shortly after his episcopal consecration, he wrote to a priest, the master of ceremonies in a certain cathedral, signing his name simply as Louis M. Martínez. As those who fill that office are accustomed to use their title in writing to all, including other bishops, this priest suggested that he should not sign his name that way but with a cross and then, Louis María, Titular Bishop of Anemurio. His Excellency answered him: "I shall sign that way when it is a matter of an official document; but when I write to my friends, I shall continue putting simply Louis M. Martínez because I am not wearing the mitre all day, seated on the episcopal throne, but there are moments when I am stretched out on the bed and raise my feet to rest, without remembering that I am a bishop."

This happy, jovial, sociable character of Archbishop Martínez dates from far back. When he was vice-rector of the seminary, he used to wait until all the students had retired to sleep, then he gathered the professors in a place apart and started them playing games and cutting capers like authentic collegians.

After these sleepless nights it was naturally very difficult to awaken Father Martínez to celebrate the six o'clock Mass, the community Mass. One of the students was assigned the duty of awakening him, and what an arduous task it was! It was a matter of struggling for fifteen or even twenty minutes to bring him back to conscious life. On one occasion the seminarian could not succeed in waking him up. It then occurred to the student to propose a syllogism that purposely had four terms.

"No conclusion!" exclaimed Father Martínez, completely awake at last.

The seminarians had a rule for judging the degree of good humor of the vice-rector: it was the position in which he wore his biretta. When he came to the chapel before six, half awake, the biretta almost covered his eyebrows. In proportion to the passage of time, the biretta gradually rose until by night he wore it almost like a zuchetto. Then the good humor of the vice-rector was at its height.

It would be endless to relate even some characteristics of the Archbishop's humor; at times it broke out almost unconsciously, even in moments that seemed most solemn. When he was canon of the cathedral in Morelia, one of the cantors, already old and whose voice quavered, intoned the psalm: "I shall sing the mercies of the Lord forever." Canon Martínez could not restrain himself and, turning to his companion, said: "Listen! What a threat!"

When consecrating a church, he was about to make the aspersions of the interior walls. He was facing the altar. The master of ceremonies reminded him that it was necessary to begin with the right side, and he pointed to the Gospel side, which was on the Archbishop's left. He, showing his right hand, said: "But this is certainly my right!"

"No, Your Excellency, that is the right." Then with a sigh of resignation, the Archbishop said: "Lord, I believe, help thou my unbelief" (Mark 9:23).

A person of slight intelligence once asked the Archbishop if he could read a certain inoffensive novel. The Archbishop, who dealt very frankly with this person, answered: "Look, you can read anything because you understand nothing."

Let us finish here or we shall go interminably.

CHAPTER III

Interior Life

THE INTERIOR LIFE of Archbishop Martínez began when he attained the use of reason, for he was very precocious, a fact proven by his remembrance of events that happened when he was scarcely three years of age. It was his mother, Ramoncita, especially, who initiated that interior life. A very pious and spiritual woman, she inculcated in her son a horror of sin and the love of God above all things.

The first personal memorandum that we have reveals the commencement of a spiritual life. The notes began in January, 1896, when he was fourteen and a half years of age. Here among interesting points about his studies, we see his care to preserve in writing the maxims that had impressed him. They are very revealing because they show us how seriously he took the spiritual life from his adolescent days, as well as the attractions or tendencies of his soul in that period. Almost all were in Latin, but we prefer to give their translation.

He who follows me does not walk in darkness (John 8:12).

Vanity of vanities, except to love God and serve him only (Eccles. 1:2).

I count all things as dung that I may gain Christ (Phil. 3:8).

Blessed are they who hunger and thirst for justice for they shall be satisfied (Matt. 5:6).

Remember that you must die.

He has filled the hungry with good things (Luke 1:53).

To him who thirsts I will give of the fountain of life freely (Apoc. 21:6).

Those who eat me still hunger (Ecclus. 24:29).

He who drinks of the water that I will give shall never thirst (John 4:14).

Just as after we taste honey, everything seems insipid; so, after we relish spiritual things, everything worldly disappoints us (St. Gregory).

We cannot have a more certain testimony of the presence of Jesus in the soul than the desire to grow in grace (St. Bernard).

On the paths of the Lord not to go forward is to go backward.

He that is just let him be justified still; he that is holy let him be sanctified more (Apoc. 22:11).

Trade till I come (Luke 19:13).

The foregoing quotations reveal the preoccupation of this youth with spiritual perfection and sanctity, as well as the foundations of his life-long hunger and thirst for God. On the Monday before Ash Wednesday of that year he writes:

Remember man that thou are dust and unto dust thou shalt return."

Be perfect as your heavenly Father is perfect (Matt. 5:8).

He who enters a contest is not crowned unless he has competed according to the rules (II Tim. 2:6).

Our whole progress and perfection lie in two things: in doing what God wishes and in doing it as he wishes us to do it (Rodríguez).

Now note well that the two following maxims, either his own or gleaned elsewhere, reveal the disposition of his soul at this period.

Die rather than offend God.

To be a great scholar, I ought to be a great saint. If I want to be holy and wise, I must be truly devoted to Mary most holy.

He who despises small things, little by little will fall (Ecclus. 19:1).

It will help us greatly to grow in virtue and perfection if we try not to commit faults deliberately (Blosius).

St. Basil gives us a means of progressing rapidly: to set our eyes on the best and on those distinguished in virtue, and try to imitate them (Rodríguez).

We must not approach the business of our progress in a general way but in particular; and it is very important to put into effect the good resolutions and desires that the Lord gives us (Rodríguez).

The saint fosters in his heart desires of ascending; the sinner, of descending (St. Jerome).

All our progress and perfection consist in doing well the individual, ordinary, daily tasks we have at hand (Rodríguez).

Have confidence and keep waiting.

We must work at the removal of our faults and imperfections in ordinary matters thus improving them daily. Let us give chief attention to this; all other considerations will be a help (Rodríguez).

All discipline and all good practices at first seem difficult, painful and sad; however, afterwards, with use they become not only easy, but very tranquil and pleasing (Rodríguez).

To the question: "Do you want to know what practice and habit do?" St. Bernard answers: "At first it seems insupportable to you; with the passage of time, you will be accustomed to it, and it will no longer seem so heavy; shortly afterwards, it will seem light to you; later on, you will not feel it at all; finally you will even take delight in it" (St. Bernard).

The road a man follows in his youth he will not abandon in his old age (Prov. 22:6).

Do not allow the good of each day to be lost and do not despise even the smallest grace (Ecclus. 14:14).

The thoughts of the soul are very prone to wander (Richard of St. Victor).

The possession of Jesus costs much because it is necessary to carry part of his cross (L. Venillot).

He who denies himself low, base and passing pleasures, disposes himself for those that are pure, spiritual and eternal (St. Augustine).

Who will find in creatures what he does not find in God, just and pure, and this with tranquillity? (St. Bernard).

Do not tire of resisting since the demon does not tire tempting you; the more troublesome the battle, the greater will be the crown (St. Lawrence Justinian).

Look at the crown that Christ offers you; he assists you and encourages you for the battle (St. Ambrose).

Although the young seminarian always lived in very protected surroundings—a pious home, country life during vacations—nevertheless it would be an error to think that his virtue was something easy and spontaneous. He had to engage in terrible combats for virtue, as we shall see later in a more relevant passage. This is proven by the fact that he notes carefully how he must struggle to conquer.

Means to avoid falling into temptation
1) To reject them the moment they are noticed.
2) To pray in the moment of temptation, protesting to God that we do not want to offend him.
3) To distract ourselves.
4) To trust in God and to distrust ourselves.
5) To bring some good thought to mind.
6) To make the temptation an occasion of doing good.

Faults that should be avoided in the struggle against temptation
1) Not to be impatient because the temptation lasts.
2) Not to be discouraged when one has the misfortune to be conquered. After conquering a temptation, we ought to thank God and prepare ourselves for the new combat.

Strategy of the devil in temptations
1) To hide the malice and ugliness of sin and to show us the pleasure it does not have.
2) To put into our mind that afterward we will confess and do penance.
3) That we can no longer resist the temptation and avoid sin.

The most experienced director could not give a more complete doctrine upon temptations. These points, doubtless, are not original, but extracted from some work.[1] It is noteworthy, at any rate, that so young a man knew how to select and summarize them so perfectly. Many years afterward, writing to a penitent, he acknowledged with simplicity that God had given him great skill in helping tempted souls.

During that same year he practiced the *Spiritual Exercises*. His resolutions are very interesting, for they also reveal the dispositions and tendencies of his soul at that age.

Resolutions from the Exercises

1) I will serve God, cost what it may, because he is my beginning and my end and my great reward.

2) I will abhor sin: on account of its punishments, its effects in my soul, and because it offends God.

3) I will avoid sin so as not to fall into the fire of hell, kindled by a just God, powerful and full of mercy.

4) I will be virtuous and *holy* in order to have a happy death, a favorable judgment and to free myself from being at Christ's left hand at the final judgment.

5) I will remain in the house of my Father, that is, in the grace of God, because it is better to be here than in the service of Satan. I want to be in the camp and under the banner of Christ; therefore I will imitate him, despising riches, pleasures, and honors, whereby I will avoid being caught in the snares of Satan and carried to his camp.

6) I will execute all that Christ asks of me, cost what it may, and I will put to work all the means that may be necessary and useful for serving God and sanctifying myself, however painful they may be, for God suffered so much for my love.

These resolutions give occasion for several observations. They reflect, of course, the *Exercises* made according to the traditional method of St. Ignatius, for they follow from the meditations on the end of man, the four last things, the kingdom of Christ, the two standards, the passion and other subjects.

---

[1] Certainly from Father Gobinet.

They indicate the seriousness and attention with which the young seminarian performed them, for he preserved the fruit of each meditation in a definite resolution which summed it up. Lastly, while they give evidence of the attempts of a beginner and the uncertain steps of a child beginning to walk, at the same time they show his insight in relating them with what was fundamental: to avoid sin at all costs and to keep himself in the grace of God.

In the *Spiritual Exercises* of 1897—he was not yet sixteen years old—a remarkable progress is noted. Here are his resolutions:

I intend to observe them efficaciously, with the divine grace, which I ask for from the Lord through the intercession of his holy Mother, of St. Ignatius and of my favorite saints, without their observance binding me under sin:

1) I shall detest and avoid, with great care and with the grace of God, mortal sin and deliberate venial sin, and I will flee from the proximate and remote occasions of sin.

2) I will make my morning prayer devoutly, thanking God for having granted me the new day, and declaring to him that I do not want to offend him during it and assuring him that I wish to employ it in his service: in the same way, by means of humble, trustful prayer, I will ask him, in the name and through the merits of Jesus Christ and of the most holy Virgin and of all the saints, especially those to whom I have the greatest devotion, to help me with his grace so that during that day I may not offend him and that I may employ it in his service. I will also offer him my heart and with it all the works of the day for his greater glory and service. At night I will say my prayers and make an examination of conscience.

3) Every morning I will make with all punctuality thirty minutes of mental prayer and I will prepare myself for it at night; I will hear Mass immediately; and at some other time during the day, I shall have spiritual reading.

4) I will be very devoted to the Virgin Mary, trying to imitate

her virtues; I will pray the Rosary every evening (at seven o'clock), I will consecrate Saturday to her, honoring her with some pious practice and light mortification; I will recommend myself to her always and I will be punctual at the Sodality meetings.

5) I will go to confession every week with due dispositions and with the purpose of advancing in virtue; and I will listen to the advice of the confessor as if coming from God and I will put it into practice.

6) I will try to be mortified and I will beg God to grant it to me; for mortification and to avoid idleness, I will devote myself to study, I will rise as soon as I am spoken to and I will observe punctually my duties and my pious practices.

7) I will try to be chaste, for which I will recommend myself to God, to the most holy Virgin and all the saints, principally during temptations, and I will try to conquer them as soon as I notice them, through means that I know and those with which God may inspire me, *cost what it may.*

8) I will try to be humble through prayer and doing what it seems to me humility requires, *cost what it may.*

9) I will not take into any account human respect and I will flee from friends and things that are dangerous, as well as idleness.

10) I will read all these promises on Communion days[2] and if I find that I am observing them, I shall thank God; and if not, I shall impose upon myself a slight penance; and at any rate I shall pray to observe them in the future.

Strengthen me in this, O Lord, in these resolutions which you yourself have inspired. My Jesus, Mary most holy, holy angels, chiefly those for whom I have greatest devotion, deign to give me grace to fulfill them. Amen. Seminary College of Morelia. Last day of Exercises, January 27, 1897. Louis M. Martínez.

No doubt, the foregoing, if regarded as resolutions, are too numerous, but it is to be understood that they are rather a plan

[2] At that time, Holy Communion was not received daily but only on Sundays and feast days. Archbishop Martínez was already a priest when St. Pius X issued the decree on frequent Communion.

of life. Positive and remarkable progress is noted among them.

Without forgetting the negative side of the spiritual life—to avoid sin at all costs—a special importance is given to the positive, to the practice of virtues, especially to three, in which Archbishop Martínez excelled: humility, purity, mortification. These will be the three columns upon which will be raised in all its magnificence, his love—love of God and of souls—which eventually will unify his whole life and perfect it in unity, according to the desire of the Master: that all may be consummated in unity.

It is to be noticed also that he has introduced into his spiritual life the traditional practices: mental prayer, daily Mass, spiritual reading, examination of conscience, weekly confession and Holy Communion as frequently as permitted at that time. And it is a matter of admiration that at such an early age he made a half hour of mental prayer daily.

Finally, he emphasizes devotion to the Blessed Virgin, for he knew well that it consists in the imitation of her virtues, and that it is nourished by the practices of piety.

The spiritual life of the Archbishop was a constant ascent. A comparison of those first resolutions of 1896 with the last that he wrote in 1954, two years before his death, impresses us. The former are a rough draft, the first lines traced by an unskilled, wavering hand; the latter are the final touches to a masterly work.

He still performed the Ignatian *Exercises* in 1955, and perhaps in 1956, because he was accustomed to devote to them the week that follows Christmas, that is, the final days of the year and the first of the New Year, but he no longer wrote, for the weakness of his eyes prevented it.

On February 14, 1915, God placed Father Martínez in contact with a soul of election; the latter was the first link in a series of chosen souls that God placed under his direction to lead them to sanctity. The meeting in 1915 was, without doubt, a providential one and the point of departure of a new stage in the spiritual life of Archbishop Martínez. Until then he certainly had been a worthy priest, but perhaps too engulfed in his philosophical studies and in seminary affairs that absorbed almost all his time. Then it became necessary to give more importance to the spiritual life.

The sanctification of a soul is a greater work than the conquest of an empire; and not only does God intervene and the soul cooperate, but ordinarily other souls help in this work. The solidarity that God has established among souls, and which in the last analysis rises from the doctrines of the Mystical Body and the communion of saints, is evidence that no one is saved alone and no one is lost alone. We all have an influence in the salvation or the perdition of our neighbor.

This holds true particularly in the ministry of spiritual direction. Although the distinctive feature is the director's influence upon the sanctification of the directed soul, nevertheless, the latter, in its turn, sometimes by example, now by prayer, again by the holy emulation awakened in the director, contributes also to his sanctification. God has willed it so.

Archbishop Martínez expounds this doctrine with his customary proficiency in a letter on Fénelon directed to his friend Canon Buitrón, in which the question is posed: "Why was not Fénelon a saint?"

Why was he not a saint? Who can fathom the secrets of souls and the hidden judgments of God?

But now that we are letting the spirit wander through the realms of the uncertain, I am going to make a daring observation. Do you remember that anecdote of a judge who used to demand in case of any misdemeanor: "Come to the point, come to the point! Who is she?" always looking for a woman in the background of all dramas?

For a long time I have thought that this question of the judge should be given whenever there is in the world some noteworthy event, something great and extraordinary whether it be for good or for evil.

Those words of Genesis: "It is not good for man to be alone; let us make him a helpmeet like to himself," are applicable not only to the institution of the family, but to all great human enterprises, inclusive of sanctity which, because it is an eminently divine undertaking, does not cease to be marvelously human.

Lemaitre himself enumerates some of those mysterious pairs: "We find near St. Jerome, a Paula or a Marcella; near St. John of the Cross, a St. Teresa; near Mme. Swetchine, a Lacordaire. . . ."

The enumeration could be continued indefinitely and even without consulting any book, but just from memory. But to what purpose? It suffices merely to point out that even in that most magnificent work of history, in the divine and human work of the Redemption, Jesus had a helpmeet like to himself, the immaculate Virgin Mary.

The interesting thing, the decisive thing for any man, is to find his helpmeet; thereupon depends his glory or his downfall.

Imagine that Fénelon, instead of finding a half-crazy woman, had met an authentic saint. Probably he would have reached sanctity in spite of his shortcomings, precisely because unsettled men who have an assemblage of contrary qualities, also have many and terrible defects; for when sanctity does not produce in a soul its work of harmony and peace, it is almost impossible for it not to have for each quality the defect that corresponds to it.

And Fénelon met Mme. Guyon precisely in the moment propitious for meetings, in full maturity, when man definitely takes his path. Before that age, neither are the defects of the man irreparable nor are his virtues absolutely fixed, excepting, of course, extraordinary cases; in youth—and that period can be prolonged greatly —he is only preparing for the trip; the equipment for beginning life's journey is packed in the suitcase; and that is the time when we begin also to hope for something without knowing what it is, but we have the inner conviction that it will come.

Meanwhile, it arrives: we make some trial flights, like aviators, until the one who is to come appears and he marks the definite course of our life. Then comes either the angel of God or the demon of midday. We can reject the one or the other because we are always free; to the one or the other we may say what the Baptist said: "Art thou he that is to come or look we for another?" Oh, how important is that moment in life! How unknown its capital importance!

Well, at that moment in Fénelon's life Mme. Guyon came; and you know the rest, how her false mysticism deceived him.

In writing the preceding, the Archbishop was speaking from his own experience. At life's maturity, God placed in his path holy souls who oriented him toward sanctity. When he met a soul whom he had to direct along the difficult path of the mystical life he, although erudite, had to confess that until then he was ignorant of this heavenly science.[3]

But conscious of his responsibility, he devoted himself earnestly to the study of mysticism. The persecution under Carranza at that time facilitated the opportunity because, with the seminary dissolved and the professors obliged to go into hiding, Father Martínez had in his refuge abundant time for study.

The first work that he read was the *Mystical Theology* of Meynard, O.P.; but he not only read attentively, he made résumés and synoptic sketches until he assimilated the doctrine perfectly. Afterward he read all the works of Garrigou-Lagrange, O.P., Gardeil, O.P., Saudreau, *Graces of Prayer* by Poulain, S.J., the mystical studies of DeGuibert, S.J., and many others. He then embarked upon those of St. John of the Cross and St. Teresa. Finally, he gave theological solidity to his work by studying St. Thomas Aquinas in what pertains to the subject.

He acquired a great competency in mysticism, as shown by his several treatises upon the Holy Spirit, soul of the mystical life: *True Devotion to the Holy Spirit; Gifts, Fruits and Beati-*

[3] Archbishop Martínez stated: "At that time I had read nothing more about mysticism than the poems of St. John of the Cross, and those from the literary point of view."

tudes; The Holy Spirit and the Interior Life; The Holy Spirit and Prayer; Secrets of the Interior Life; and numerous others.

Later on he turned to advantage the persecution of 1926 to 1929, during which it was again necessary to be hidden, by writing a synthesis of all his knowledge of mysticism. In this work, still unpublished, he makes use not only of his speculative knowledge, but also of the experimental, acquired sometimes from other souls, sometimes from his own soul.

Although it is not easy to establish with certain precision the stages of the Archbishop's spiritual life, because on this subject he was extraordinarily reserved, nevertheless, I can point them out in their general lines.

February 14, 1915. First meeting, truly providential, with the first soul of election.

February 14, 1916. He takes charge formally of the aforesaid soul, after having understood that such was the will of God.

September 21, 1916. God promises him that he will attain the transforming union.

October 7, 1916. Consecration, full surrender to God, indicating a new stage in his spiritual life. This is what is customarily called "the second conversion."

Then follows a long period of twelve years in which he suffered the passive purifications, indispensable for arriving at infused contemplation. According to all probabilities, (a) God combined in this period, as he is accustomed to do at times, both nights, that of the senses and that of the spirit; (b) during this period there were some alternations: it was not all dryness and aridity; but desolation predominated, and prolonged, terrifying, temptations, particularly in the first years.

Before enlarging on this point, we should recall that there are many kinds of temptations: those that come from the devil, the world and our own inclination to evil. Restricting ourselves to those that come from the devil, they can be of two classes:

ordinary temptations, proper to the ascetical life, with which
the devil annoys good souls, and can be overcome by the ordinary grace of God; and extraordinary temptations, proper to
the mystical life, which give an occasion to practice virtue in a
heroic degree. These temptations are one of the principal instruments of the passive purifications; they cannot be overcome
except by an extraordinary grace of God.

How far, how very far, are we ordinary Christians from
understanding the temptations of holy souls! If we did know
them, we would be scandalized, because we harbor the miscon-
ception that holy souls are sheltered from the devil's attacks,
and that since they live in a heavenly atmosphere, no breath
of the evil one may touch them.

Very different is the reality. Saints are persons of great contrasts. We see it in Christ himself, supreme model of all sanctity. In his soul, as in a mirror, the divine light of the beatific
vision and of infused knowledge was ever shining, but sometimes the sky became cloudy and the storm broke out. What
surges of grief, even to tears; of sadness, even to death; of loath-
ing, even to bloody sweat! The heart of Christ was a heaven of
joy and an ocean of sorrow.

The heart of the saints is something like that. How many
times they experience heaven in their soul: the divine light of
contemplation floods them, celestial peace inundates them, the
love of God incloses them with that embrace which, if it were
not fleeting, would cause their death. And immediately, almost
without transition, the tempest follows furiously, the sky is
obscured, faith seems extinguished, hope shines no longer, love
is dead, as it were; and at the same time, all the passions are
unchained; everything seems a sham and a lie; desperation
crushes them; hate and blasphemy besiege them; anger, glut-
tony, lust are converted into wild beasts against which it now
seems useless to struggle.

And when the storm passes away, the delicacy of the soul is

a new torment. In anguish it asks, "Have I offended God in the least?" But, when God wills it, he commands the winds and there comes a great calm and deep peace and tranquillity reign again.

Archbishop Martínez will show us all this with his own words. On March 1, 1926, he writes as follows in his personal notes:

I discover three conditions for perfect love:

It must be *total:* one must love with his whole heart, with his whole soul and with all his strength. To love is to concentrate one's whole being and entire life in a single giving, which has something of immensity.

It must be *singular;* the word "love" has no plural; one can love only one single thing; if the giving that constitutes love must be total, it cannot be made except once. Is this not the supreme attraction of love? To concentrate our being and life on one single point —this is to love.

It must be *eternal* by its nature; the gift of love is made one single time, it lasts forever. It must be something definitive and irrevocable.

Thus God loves himself in the mystery of his life. Thus he loves each one of us in the mystery of his mercy. God loves me totally with his infinite being and with his eternal life; nor can he love me in any other way because he is himself simplicity and Love.

Shall I dare to say that he loves me as his *only one?* I shall not understand how, but it must be so. My heart demands it that way; and he made my heart. Love is like that. God loves other creatures, no doubt, but he loves each one of them as if he had nothing else to love; especially souls, because the love which he has for them is that of a spouse and such love is for one only. Mysteries of love!

And his love is eternal: "I have loved you with an everlasting love" (Jer. 31:3). He has loved me eternally. He will love me eternally. I want to love him that way, too. I want to concentrate my being and my life, my whole being and my whole life in him who is my only one and I want to make him the one, eternal gift of love.

There is something of the immense in love. Before my eyes and before my heart is all: God and the universe. The glance of my intelligence has something of the infinite because its object is being; the beating of my heart has something of the infinite because its object is the good. Through the gift of my love I fold up, like gigantic fans, the glances of my intellect, which can be extended out to all things, and the affections of my heart, which can love all, in order to concentrate my gaze upon one thing only: for him; and to simplify my affections into one alone: his love.

When God's gift and mine, now perfected, meet and blend, the mystery of love is accomplished. God will be I and I will be God, not by exchange of natures, which would be heresy, but by the transformation of love. Or rather, God will live in me and I in him. When will that perfect transformation which God has promised me be completed?

O Mary, you advanced the hour of Jesus at Cana of Galilee; advance God's hour for me, the hour of my complete transformation, so that the muddy water of my being may be changed into exquisite wine, that is, into your Son, Jesus.

Today was a day of love. During the morning I felt the entrancing presence of God, his call, as it were, to one distracted by occupations. In the afternoon, I commenced prayer by an impetuous impulse of love and during all of it I only loved so ardently that I was not able to do more. It seemed to me that the love did not fit into my breast; I surrendered myself to Jesus totally, as if I should like to pour into one point my being and my life so as to cast it into his heart. I cannot come near expressing what I experienced this day. Loving desires . . . the disquiet of one who has caught a glimpse of happiness but does not attain it.

One day, upon beginning prayer, I happened to think: If I should ask Jesus this question: "Do you love me?" . . . I did not express it, but the thought moved me. In that question this affirmation is implied: "I love you!" But I did not dare to ask the question; I felt my unworthiness and it made me ashamed.

During the afternoon, my heart was inflamed with an ardent love. Now, indeed, I told myself, I am going to love God; I am going to begin to love him. I wanted a new way of loving, as it were, because everything seemed too little for loving him. I went out for a ride in a car and during the entire time love burned in my heart and my thought frequently went out to God. What shall I do to love him? I surrendered myself to him at each instant with my whole being and my whole life, and I repeated the "Offering"[4] slowly and affectionately.

I am entirely resolved to do nothing else in my life but to love, to change everything into love. It seems to me that little by little all earthly things are losing their attractiveness and that I no longer seek nor desire nor find interest in anything but to love. To love in prayer, in work, in sacrifice. To love even with the most commonplace actions of my life. Henceforth, I shall do nothing else but love.

A certain affair made me understand that I am fading out before men, that I am regarded as inadequate; and perhaps for the first time I felt the joy of disappearing. The "love to be unknown and to be reputed as nothing"[5] was revealed under a new aspect, the aspect of love. May my eyes see nothing but him; may no eyes see me but his. Seeing seems just as contrary to love as being seen if outside the circle of love's unity.

Love is solitude. God lives in infinite solitude, in divine isolation. The Father and the Son love each other in the unity of the Holy Spirit. The mystery of love is accomplished in the soul's aloneness, or rather, perhaps, in God's aloneness. Lord, when shall you and I be completely alone?

Today I made Jesus a total surrender of my being and of my life; since I am all his, I shall be all the Father's.

That God may communicate himself to a soul it is necessary that the soul be in absolute peace; everything that disturbs peace, however legitimate it may be, hinders communication with God. Thanks to him, I am in peace in the midst of the terrible tempest unleashed against us.[6] I feel a strength, an indifference, a tranquillity that I recognize as a very special grace of God.

[4] The Archbishop is referring to a formula with which he made one of his many "surrenders."

[5] Cf. *Imitation of Christ.*

[6] Reference to the religious persecution of 1926 to 1929.

Epochs of persecution decidedly suit me. In 1914 I lived a new life through the influence exercised upon me by a holy soul. Now I am living as in heaven. With what delicacy God treats me! He inebriates me with love in the midst of the storm, as a mother who fondles and caresses her child to keep him from being frightened. No doubt, God treats me thus lest I abandon him through my weakness in the hour of trial.

Or can it be that in each persecution some soul is suffering so that I may be in peace? The union of souls is so real and deep, that when God has united them, they are like one single thing; and the portion of pain and of joy which the hand of God must pour out into them, he distributes in such a way that the strong, holy soul suffers all the pain, and the weak, imperfect soul receives all the peace. At any rate, blessed be God! His will is as holy, as wise, as loving when he inflicts pain as when he caresses; when he immolates on the cross as when he inebriates with love.

I wish to live in peace, because God wishes that I so live. Why lose peace? My treasure, my only treasure, my infinite treasure, my God and our mutual love, neither anything nor anyone can snatch away from me; and that treasure suffices to make me happy. All that the persecutors do to me: confiscations, prison, outrages, even death, will do nothing else than increase my treasure and give me more perfect possession of it.

One thing would disturb me: that Mexico should lose the faith. But I am sure that God will not abandon it because it is the nation of Mary of Guadalupe. This persecution, like those preceding, will make its faith more deeprooted and strengthen it, as the oaks of our forests are strengthened when the hurricane agitates them. And if—may God forbid—he allows my fatherland to lose its faith, my broken heart must conform to that sovereign will.

The persecution is a grace of God, a blessing from God, a beatitude, and Jesus taught us that our attitude in persecution is expressed with these two words: "Gaudete et exultate!"

In the afternoon, first, impatience for the time of prayer; as soon as I knelt before the altar, my spirit was held fixed upon Jesus, my soul burning in his love. It was a greater impression than that of the preceding days.

In a singular manner I saw in Jesus an irresistible attraction, like something superior to what has hitherto appealed to my heart, a something that did not fit into my soul, something so sweet that I could not come near relishing its sweetness, so great that it was impossible to embrace it, so new that I had never before suspected it. And what my spirit saw, evoked in my heart a new love also, which my breast could not contain. There was something overflowing as much in the spirit as in the heart. I felt some relief in surrendering myself to Jesus as a slave of love. . . .

In the morning, my soul was fixed in God in soothing recollection. During the day, eagerness for purity and inclination toward God. In the evening, in the prayer which exceeded the usual time because I could not separate myself from Jesus, the same impression as yesterday, but deeper and more heavenly.

The *intuition of Jesus* (at any rate I must call it that), vague yet profound, shows Jesus to me as something unique, above everything, that attracts me in an irresistible way. There is no similarity between this impression and ordinary impressions and perceptions. Jesus does not fit into my understanding; I discern him as immense; and it is natural, for he is God; I perceive him as inexhaustible, he fills and satisfies the spirit, but I have a sense of inadequacy. I cannot stop looking at him; I feel repose and consolation in being with him, while a certain trembling reaches even the body.

The impulse of love which belongs to intuition was less impetuous today, but more precise, more robust, more solid. I need a new heart for this love. I am beginning to feel what it is to have placed one's eyes and one's heart so high; eyes and heart are delightfully inadequate for so lofty an object. A *renovation* of soul is indispensable.

Upon delivering myself to Jesus under the loving impulse evoked by the singular intuition, it seemed to me that giving him my whole being is very little as that reaction does not correspond to the action. It is necessary to give more; to give myself entirely is the height of human love; but to this higher love a new giving must correspond.

I see that the love of God demands the total gift of ourselves and of other souls (love of neighbor is the natural complement of love of God); and still more, the perfection of divine love requires us to love with the heart of God, to love with the Holy Spirit.[7]

It seemed to me also—can it be an illusion?—that upon loving Jesus thus I felt *a strange* impulse, like a current dragging me along, and therefore, perhaps, the reaction of my soul seemed so small. If the Holy Spirit breathes, only he can make the gift of love vibrate to his impulse.

Today, as yesterday, I went to my rest to offer myself and to hand myself over to Jesus as a *slave of love*. How much is contained in those words! One who loves is satisfied only by that full, absolute surrender which is signified by slavery. May my whole being, my whole life belong to him, may I be in his hands and may those adorable hands give me life or death.

To love is to lose liberty, but not in the relative manner as the ancient slaves lost it, but in an absolute manner, which is abandonment. To love is to feel the happiness of losing liberty!

Stability in God intellectually. I note the difference when the intellect or the will attends to God. . . .

In the morning prayer, the intellect attends to God with recollection. In the afternoon, prayer of love more impetuous, more ardent, more sensible than in the preceding days. An irresistible and indescribable impulse toward Jesus which made me weep . . .; a desire of effacing myself, of dying. There is a very close relationship between love and death. *To love* is, in a certain sense, *to die*.

While travelling in an auto, I felt that God was attracting me in the interior of my heart, that he was uniting me with himself, that I was enjoying his love; and I experienced a very sweet desire to suffer, but a suffering intrinsic to love.

One cannot love without suffering. He who loves, feels the necessity of giving himself and he sees that the gift and the suffering are one and the same thing.

[7] A common expression among the mystics. To love with the heart of God or to love with the Holy Spirit is to love with the infused love that belongs to infused contemplation.

Anyone who understands something of mysticism will discover in these lines the characteristics of contemplation and of infused love.

Archbishop Martínez frequently preached upon the subject of miseries. This is truly an unattractive theme, yet it is a very profitable one for souls. He used to repeat at each step that we should not be embarrassed by our miseries nor discouraged to see ourselves miserable. Miseries are not an obstacle to our sanctification; on the contrary, if we know how to profit by them, they are an indispensable and most efficacious means for arriving at sanctity.

For a proper understanding, let us begin by clarifying the meaning of the term, "miseries." Some miseries are of the physical order: the ignorance of our mind, so limited in knowledge; the weakness of our will, so given to vascillating; the inconstancy of our fickle heart; the blemishes of our body; illness and spells of exhaustion. One person suffers the consequences of lowly origin and deficient education, which leave a roughness and rudeness never completely eradicated. Another has some impulsive movements or nervous twitching which frequently exposes him to ridicule. But the list would be interminable. We might rather ask ourselves, "What can we do in which there is not some deficiency, some imperfection, some defect?" Neither in walking nor in speaking, neither in gestures nor in the simplest actions. Only Jesus did all things well.

Other miseries are of the moral order and these are incomparably more numerous and of greater weight. Beyond a doubt, grave sin and even all voluntary sin is the great moral misery, or rather, the only one. But in treating of miseries from this special point of view, we do not include mortal sin directly, nor even fully deliberate venial sin, especially the habitual.

Moral miseries are: the humiliation that the commission of sin brings with it, even when we have been fully purified from those sins; the inclination to evil that, although dominated, always makes new falls possible; temptations that humble us deeply and make us skirt the brink of sin; semi-deliberate faults and imperfections; and during pious exercises, especially in prayer, the wandering of the mind, sleep, aridity, helplessness and the like.

Misery thus considered is not an evil, but a good, if we know how to use it. How may we utilize miseries? Miseries serve:

1. *To know ourselves.* Self knowledge, the basis of humility, is not acquired with theories nor speculations, but by feeling our misery experimentally. And if the gift of knowledge intervenes and in its light we sound the abyss of our wretchedness, we remain healed forever of our foolish conceit. Then flattery will try in vain to elevate us to the clouds or calumny to plunge us into the mire, the soul cannot be elated with praise nor be wounded with injuries; it will remain steadfast in humility.

2. *To exercise humility* and to grow in this fundamental, necessary virtue. Humility is practiced only with humiliation; and what greater humiliation than to feel the weight of our miseries? Humiliations from outside, those caused by our fellow man, are small compared with those that rise from ourselves.

3. *To serve as a counterbalance* to natural gifts, such as success, praise, honors and especially to supernatural gifts, graces and heavenly favors. Without that balance, we would lose equilibrium and fall pitifully.

4. Principally, *to draw upon ourselves the mercy of God.* What can attract mercy but misery? The mercy of God is not pity, it is love; it is the garb with which love clothes itself so as to love the miserable.

Are not these motives sufficient to keep us from being distressed by our wretchedness and, still more, to bring us eventually to love it? Jesus was the first to love our limitations; and he loved them so much that he clothes himself in them: "Wherefore, it was right that he should in all things be made like unto his brethren" (Heb. 2:17).

Archbishop Martínez preached so much about miseries that a religious gave him an appellation, which, far from being disrespectful, paid him a great compliment. She called him the "Lord of Miseries." To understand this title, one must know the Mexican custom of calling the most venerated images of Jesus Crucified by the name, "Lord of so and so," for example, "Lord of Pardon," "Lord of Expiation." Therefore, she called Archbishop Martínez "Lord of Miseries," which is tantamount to saying "Lord of Mercy and Forbearance."

But this doctrine was not a theory; he learned it in the school of his own bitter experience. Let us continue gleaning from his personal notes of this period, in order to confirm, as we said before, this mixture of light and shadow in the Archbishop's soul; the latter more dense in the early years of this period, the former, more abundant in the final years.

Many miseries today, the chief one being that I felt a little preoccupied with the judgments of men.

Yesterday I was overwhelmed with work. Perhaps on this account or because of yesterday's failings, my soul was in aridity. It is very just, I say to God, that you chastise me; I place myself in your hands. In the afternoon, prayer always dry, but a very deep recollection possessed me. What can it be?

At night upon taking leave of the Blessed Sacrament, a little worried about the religious persecution, I said to Jesus: At least in these difficult circumstances do not abandon me! I was referring to the aridity of that entire day. But at once I thought: No, better to wish to be as you have me, better to wish to do your most holy will.

And with deep emotion I surrendered myself to his good pleasure, feeling the joy of pleasing him, joy that in me he may do what he wishes. O ineffable bliss of doing the divine will! The aridity disappeared and my soul was bathed in peace and union.

There is something better than to feel God's sweet presence, it is to please him in aridity and in suffering. The supreme thing in human life is to surrender to the divine will. To wish totally and perfectly what God wishes is to resemble God as perfectly as possible.

At the end of 1922, the Holy See entrusted to Father Martínez the government of the diocese of Chilapa[8] as Apostolic Administrator. The mission was a delicate and difficult one. Father Martínez, who until then had governed only his seminary, knew how to act with such tact and prudence, that in a few months all was ready so that the new bishop could take possession.

On April 14, 1923, he wrote to a friend: "I am about to sing the *Nunc dimittis* in this land and await the new orders of the Master. It is so secure, so pleasing, and so comfortable to be in those powerful, loving hands!"

The new order was the appointment of Father Martínez as Auxiliary Bishop of Morelia, on June 6, 1923. In this connection we quote two very revealing letters.

Chilapa, June 29, 1923

My very dear friend,

Your letter of the 25th instant moved me. May God reward you and may he preserve for me your holy friendship.

I am definitely resolved to make the *Exercises* in that house, where there is truly all that I need. There I shall prepare myself to receive "strength from on high" on my approaching Pentecost.

I have asked myself in amazement: Why should God wish to elevate me to the plenitude of the priesthood? I found the answer in those words of Jesus which enclose the mystery of the episcopate as told to the apostles, whose successors are the bishops: "You

[8] Father Martínez was in Chilapa from December 6, 1922, until September, 1923. At that time, when there was no air travel, communication with Chilapa was very difficult and the town could be reached only by horseback. Consequently, Chilapa lived as in another century. His appointment as Apostolic Administrator completely upset his life and disorganized his family, though his mother felt it her duty to accompany him.

shall receive power when the Holy Spirit comes upon you and you shall be witnesses for me."[9] A new outpouring of the Holy Spirit! To be witness to Jesus! Witnesses of Jesus who, unknown and despised, now has so great need of testimony!

But it is strange, very strange, that God wants to grant me that dignity, which does not fit into the narrowness of my misery. You do not know this misery,[10] but I know it and God knows it better. Nevertheless, he desires me to be bishop; and in order to relieve me of all scruple, he willed that, contrary to custom, they did not ask me for my consent. He has always worked that way with me.

When I was lacking the experience and maturity of age, he assigned me to the great work of the seminary. Although I had no knowledge of sociology, he placed me at the head of a great work of social reconstruction. Being absolutely incapable of direction, I received in my clumsy hands a choice soul. Without a knowledge of canon law and never having been in a curia, I came to govern a most difficult diocese. Now, laden with miseries, I am going to receive the sacred dignity. Always the same, always the same!

Therefore, I am going to select as the legend on my coat of arms those words of St. Paul: *Cum infirmor, tunc potens sum.*[11] How does that seem to you? To symbolize the mystery, I shall place on the escutcheon a simple cross, for it is the best emblem of the mystery; or if it is desirable to express it in a somewhat more decorative form, it will be a tender vine clinging to an oak.

I have two hopes (in reality only one) that calm me completely: the depth of my misery and the divine efficacy of that Spirit who transformed the twelve into apostles.

Only to you do I speak so intimately, but enough for the present.

---

[9] Acts 1:8.

[10] When ordinary persons speak of *miseries,* we must not think that they use it in the same sense. Sinners speak of miseries when referring to a sinful, disordered life. Holy souls speak of miseries in the sense that we have explained. If they refer to sins, they deal rather with those they could commit if God had not preserved them by his grace.

[11] II Cor. 12:10: When I am weak, then am I powerful.

Chilapa, August 31, 1923

My dear friend,

I cannot resist the temptation to answer your letter of August 27, which touched me to the heart because it has a soul, a rare thing in letters, because those who write them either do not have that spiritual breath or they do not allow it to be felt; they lack simplicity. . . .

Perhaps you are right in saying that the mystery of weakness is the initial word. I am in doubt, because the Eucharist, which is the last word, is the supreme manifestation of that mystery, and because I read someplace—you know where!—that the union of the Word with the soul, the final word on earth of the spiritual life, is realized at the point where both abysses are united: the abasement of the Word and the abasement of the soul. But whether first or last, the mystery of weakness is my *word,* my way, my program.

At one time, I had selected the legend that you had proposed to me; now I am strongly attached to my own. Probably it is because the years not only cheer one up, as you say, but that they also give us the deep, vivid impression of our misery, or rather, perhaps, because in the prime of life one seeks more than a beautiful thought, as in youth, more than a sweet remembrance, as in old age; one seeks a program of life, of action, through the pressing demands of the present.

The daring word of St. Paul, *Cum infirmor, tunc potens sum,* includes two parts: in the second, *I am powerful,* the whole mystery of Christ is in us; the intensity of the interior life, the fecundity of the apostolic life, all that the Lord wishes to do by means of his *faithful servant.* But the first part is the condition, the way, the program which I ought to follow. If I humble myself, my life will be Christ; if I submerge myself in my profound wretchedness, God will do with me whatsoever he desires.

It does not concern me to mark out my mission: he knows what he wants of me. He has determined the measure of my power and my action. It is my role to bury myself so as to be able to cry out to him *De profundis,* to hear his voice resounding in the abyss and to receive his strength together with his mission: *tunc potens sum.*

On the other hand, I have no fear of forgetting that Christ is my life but I do indeed fear forgetting that I am nothing. It is hard to believe; we do forget this with greater facility in spite of its evident midday clarity; and more so in certain circumstances.

I wish, finally, that my legend and my whole escutcheon have the living, irradicable fragrance of the charm of divine love; and if it embodies the mystery of weakness, no one can doubt its origin and its relations.

I have sent the model to X so that he may order it made; as a base I used Monsignor Darboy's design: a silver cross upon an azure field; the labarum of Constantine must have shone like that against the blue of the sky. But something Mexican had to be placed there or rather something Marian; so I placed in the four quadrants left free by the cross, four roses, those of Tepeyac, which also includes the mystery of weakness. Over the cross and the roses, crowning the shield, the Holy Spirit will soar, *Virtus altissimus;* thus completing the symbolism with something that cannot be forgotten on an episcopal coat of arms.

The Holy Spirit is the Perfecter: Perfecter of the mystery of God, of the mystery of Christ, of the mystery of the Christian life, of the mystery of the priesthood. The Christian life is an *effusion* of the Holy Spirit, a *union* with the Word, a *consecration* to the Father. Likewise, too, the mystery of the priesthood: it is an effusion of the Holy Spirit. Upon conferring the diaconate, the bishop says: *Accipe Spiritum Sanctum ad robur* . . . ; upon conferring the priesthood, *Accipe Spiritum Sanctum, quorum remiseris* . . . ; upon consecrating a bishop, *Accipe Spiritum Sanctum,* without limitations. These effusions unite our souls more and more closely to Christ, the Priest; and through him, with him, in him, they consecrate us for the ministry *in gloriam Patris.* How much might be said upon this! How could the Holy Spirit be forgotten on a bishop's coat of arms?[12]

With these dispositions, Father Martínez received the epis-

[12] Letters to J.G.T. The motto which he had proposed was: *Mihi vivere Christus est.*

copal consecration, Sunday, September 30, 1923, in the cathedral of Morelia, with all the splendor of the sacred liturgy. Archbishop Leopoldo Ruiz was consecrator and the co-consecrators were Bishop Francisco Banegas, Bishop of Querétaro, and Bishop Leopoldo Lara, Bishop of Tacámbaro.

After his consecration, Bishop Martínez devoted himself to collaborating intelligently and selflessly with the great Archbishop Ruiz, who was accustomed to call him "my Cyrenean."

On July 7, 1924, God placed in the hands of Bishop Martínez the direction of an exceptional soul, Señora Concepión Cabrera de Armida. He began by giving her some spiritual exercises; and from then until her death, it was an annual occurrence. Besides verbal communication, he used to give her written points daily. The exercises were prolonged, lasting almost a month. The manuscript of each one of these retreats could form many volumes. Finally, he maintained a copious correspondence with Señora Armida; those letters could also form several volumes.

It is a matter of wonder that His Excellency found time for all this work, without neglecting in the least his important responsibilities. But more wonderful still are the torrents of light that those writings contained. No one understood the doctrine of the Cross as did Bishop Martínez. He was God's instrument to give the final, masterly touches to her soul. He knew how to impress upon her convincing motives to carry her to the loftiest heights of perfection.

At the same time, the doctrine of the Cross had a decisive influence in the sanctification of His Excellency himself. He assimilated its spirit and lived its life, thus finishing his preparation for the central grace of March 25 and of September 27, 1927.

Archbishop Martínez not only helped Señora Armida, but he

also promoted the "Works of the Cross" initiated by her.[13] Several times he gave the retreats to the Missionaries of the Holy Spirit. On one occasion when only one member asked him to give the retreat, he did not disdain to give it to him alone as if he were dealing with a large group. Innumerable are his exhortations to the Religious of the Cross through the *Spiritual Exercises,* retreats and conferences in different houses, although this involved long trips. He directed many religious, sometimes verbally, sometimes by correspondence, among them, Mother Manuela Cacho Ordozgoiti, who died with a reputation for sanctity.

He also assisted the Alliance of Love in its various centers. When Father Felix,[14] trying to reorganize the Apostolic League, grouped together several priests and called them "Priests of the Holy Spirit," Father Martínez was among them. He was the first Director of the Apostolate of the Holy Spirit when Father Felix founded it in Morelia, August 20, 1917.

Finally, soon after the death of Señora Armida, he came to the Primatial See of Mexico, and with all his authority he continued supporting and protecting the Works of the Cross, although he knew that they had many powerful enemies. He was not timid in declaring that those works were very dear to his heart.

How great was his fidelity! And the more so, since through human weakness and limitations, he did not always meet the understanding and gratitude he deserved. One year before his death, he introduced the diocesan processes of Father Felix and Señora Armida for their beatification and canonization. To the last days of his life, he kept informed of the progress of those processes.

[13] The Works of the Cross are five: the Apostolate of the Cross, the Religious of the Cross of the Sacred Heart, the Alliance of Love, the Apostolic League, the Missionaries of the Holy Spirit (*Trans.*).

[14] Father Felix Rougier, founder of the Congregation of the Missionaries of the Holy Spirit (*Trans.*).

CHAPTER IV

Lights of Contemplation

LET US CONTINUE the account of the development of Archbishop Martínez' spiritual life from his personal notes.

In today's Mass, a deep emotion through the mutual giving between Jesus and my soul. Jesus gave himself over to me—oh supreme delight!—and I delivered myself to him, through Eucharistic Communion. Tears poured from my eyes; my soul was wrapped in holy emotion.

In the afternoon, during the walk which I have been accustomed to take these last Sundays and during which a grace of God is never lacking, I felt a deeply interior peace and a delightful satisfaction in doing the will of God. During those moments I wanted nothing except to be unconditionally in accord with God's will, in my interior life as well as in exterior things. My only ambition, my only desire, my only happiness, is that the divine will may be fulfilled in me, that God may do with me whatever pleases him, that he may dispose of all that I am and all that I have, with the sovereign liberty of the beloved.

During the night I felt the ardent force of love; something that did not fit into my heart and which moved my whole being; an indefinable impression, deep and sweet, carrying me to God; a suffering that burned me; an impatience that tortured me; a tenderness that made me weep. Never had I experienced so ardent and so sensible a love.

It is not superfluous to note that all we have seen as well as what we shall see afterwards pertains not to the sensible fervor of beginners, but to the abundance and overflow of the spiritual fervor of perfect charity. The Archbishop, with his accustomed competency, explains to us these relations between sensibility and the love of God. In a letter to a friend, commenting on the verse, "My heart and my flesh have rejoiced in the living God" (Ps. 83:3), he says:

But I discover something more in that text. It seems very certain to me that sensibility plays its part in love for God, a more important part than one thinks at first sight. Here are the stages through which, in my judgment, sensibility progresses.

1) In the beginning, sensibility has a share in one's love for God that belongs to it by the very nature of man, granted that the supernatural act is grafted with the natural, psychological act.

2) Afterwards, sensibility endeavors to participate more in the spiritual acts of the soul; but it does so in a coarse way, hindering, rather than helping, the perfection of the act. Here we place certain troublesome disturbances that affect some highly emotional temperaments.[1]

3) In the third stage the connection of body and spirit is lost, so to speak; the latter is elevated, the former has no nourishment.[2]

4) Afterwards comes a moment—the fourth stage—in which the connection is resumed, but in an inverse sense: it is not the sensible part which prepares and arouses the spiritual; it is the latter which, by its richness and plenitude, is poured out on the inferior part, spiritualizing it, so to speak.

How shall I make my meaning clear? It is no longer the imagination which presents to the understanding the fecund image that prepares for the concept; but, from the sumptuous banquet of the soul, there falls to the imagination morsels more strengthening than the dainty foods that nature offers.

It is no longer the sensitive appetite that draws the will or makes its movements sensible; it is the will that, in its divine impulse, attracts the appetite, as it were, to a spiritual region.

[1] Hence the need of the passive purifications that transform and spiritualize sensibility.

[2] State of dryness.

This is the verification of the deep, beautiful expression, "My heart and my flesh exult!"[3]

Father Martínez found himself at this stage.

I spent these days recollected and full of love, even when in the street. The most noteworthy thing was a prayer in which I considered the Word of God in Jesus, but so vivid and intimate that I cannot express it. I felt how unfathomable is his majesty and how captivating his beauty. It attracted me, it drew me, making on my heart a sweet, yet mildly sad impression.[4]

That beauty, which I felt without seeing, subdues and humbles. The only attitude that the soul can take, and which it sees itself obliged to take in the presence of beauty, is abasement, but the abasement of love. Beauty humbles; perhaps even created beauty. But what one not only contemplates but loves is beauty stepped down out of love.

Can it be that consideration of all the divine attributes humbles, but that each attribute effects a lowering with its own proper tint, which in the case of beauty is the tint of love? Or is it, perhaps, that all deep consideration of God humbles and enamors; humbles because God is infinite; enamors because God is love?

This sweet, deep impression, although at one time it was more intense, had its preparation and its consequences: it was the theme of these days.

On the feast of the Incarnation, God inspired Bishop Martínez to make a loving, total consecration to Jesus Christ through the hands of Mary Immaculate. Without knowing it, he was thereby preparing himself for the central grace which he would receive one year afterwards on the same date. That grace was no other, as far as we can judge, than the transforming union, which some months later—September 21, 1927—was confirmed with a special seal of spiritual fecundity. On Good Friday, 1926, he writes:

[3] Letter of November 3, 1920, to J.G.T.
[4] The mystics call this "obscure contemplation."

Sensible devotion, even to tears, at Mass. I relished the verses of the *"Stabat Mater."* Very recollected during the day. At night, while praying the Divine Office, I felt God in the interior of my soul, so real, so united to me, that I could scarcely continue the prayer. I felt God, who did not fit into my heart; God, who filled my soul with gladness and love!

To the sweet intimacy that seized my soul, was joined a bitterness proper to love, or rather, that inexplicable, loving sadness. Can it be that love dilates desire, and that desire is impatient and unquiet? Can it be that the soul is inadequate for divine love and that the consciousness of its inadequacy torments it while it loves?

During the following days, that grace continued and kept developing ardently and intimately.

God always with me in prayer, united with my soul. At times it overwhelms me, at times I rest in him, at times that intimate union enraptures my heart. To be united with him! *To possess him!*

April 1, Holy Thursday. Day of love and of sorrow. Mass very devout. Agitated day. At night from eleven o'clock until twelve, adoration before the repository: although overcome with fatigue, I could be recollected.

April 2, Good Friday. Office very devotional. In the morning, I meditated on the Victim's Way of the Cross. In the afternoon at three o'clock, a simple, pious inauguration of the *Sacerdotal Union;* another Way of the Cross, very refreshing.

April 3. Holy Saturday. I preached upon the solitude of the Blessed Virgin. Here are the ideas:

Love is realized in a magnificent solitude. Love is strong as death, because it draws and detaches the soul and throws it into an incomprehensible solitude. Love despoils one of everything: of things, of persons, of self.

Insofar as we think about ourselves, to that extent relics of our egoism remain in us, perfect love does not rule us.

He who loves has eyes only for the Beloved, he has neither heart nor life except for him. For one who loves, the entire universe revolves around the Beloved; for him, flowers scatter their fragrance, the mountains serve him as a grandiose pedestal; the waters of the river murmur his name and the stars of the firmament write it with their light.

When the soul becomes completely emptied, Jesus comes to fill it; but when he disappears, what must that solitude be?

What must the solitude of the Blessed Virgin have been? Something worse than hell; because the torment of the reprobate is solitude without love; the torment of Mary is solitude with an immense, unique love.

Two words, deeply meaningful, vividly intimate, fill the week: *Yours—Mine.*

The dear God whom I feel in my soul since Good Friday, has drenched it during this week with his greatness and his love. Sometimes, in the street, the deep impression has overwhelmed me and I have made my way like a somnambulist. On other occasions, the impetuous, rich love of my heart has overflowed through my lips, exhausting the poor lexicon of love expressed in human speech. But the two words mentioned express the dominant emotions.

Yours; I have spoken it to him in all tones and I have put into this word my being and my life. *Yours* my body, my soul, my present, my future. *Yours* for all that you may wish to do with me. *Yours* for the intimate operations of my soul. *Yours* to work for you. *Yours* to be immolated by you.

Totally yours, surrendered to all the dispositions of your will. Yours to caress me and yours to condemn me. Yours to give me life and yours to give me death.

Sometimes I have placed myself before him in an expectant attitude, disposed for *anything. Yours* is the word of love and within it I have caught sight of limitless depths.

But another word, enrapturing and divine, has also sounded in my soul: *Mine! Mine! Mine!*

Mine; Jesus, the Word of God made flesh; *mine,* that God whom I bear in my soul and to whom I have surrendered myself in an excess of love!

Sometimes, and one day especially, it seemed that he said to me in a very emphatic way: *I love you! I love you!* How is it that I did not die of love?

And when that word was uttered, he became more closely bound with my soul; when I said to him; I love you! my soul was united still more closely with the sweet Beloved.

Mine! Is it possible? Forty-odd years of my life had to pass away before I could feel the supreme delight of his word of love and before I could say mine in the sincerity, the intimacy, the ardor of my tenderness. Thanks, my God! *You, mine;* and *I, Yours.* The solemn, sacred hour of love has struck for my soul!

Today the holy delight of those two mystic words, *Yours* and *mine,* came to a climax. Today I felt myself so much his, and I felt him so much mine, that I disappeared, as it were, while he filled my whole being. Can it be a forecast of the divine transformation?

Such it was, in fact. The grace of the transforming union does not come at one stroke. It begins by degrees, just as the dawn begins the new day, and developing, changes into the splendors of noonday brightness. But there is this difference, the sun declines toward its setting, while that grace continues increasing and producing its fruits, until transformed into the eternal splendor.

How many times in prayer I have repeated the word *Master.* I have plunged myself into the unfathomable delight of this word of love: *I have a Master!*

To have Jesus as Master is like a beginning of eternal felicity. I long for him to exercise over me, free and fully, his rights as Master, especially, as Master through love, as Master because I selected him from millions to be my owner.

May he not console me, may he not hold me of any account, let him be my *Owner.* And I, shall I dare to be his owner?

The excessive work of Lent brought on some days of illness. He then had neither time nor strength to do anything but accept the will of God practically and to say to him: *"I am yours."* When his health was finally restored, the graces of God returned also.

At the foot of the altar, I felt myself intimately united to Jesus and, binding myself to him ardently, I surrendered myself to him saying: *I am yours,* but putting a new meaning into this phrase.

It was a complete giving in which my being faded away, so to speak. *I want to be yours,* I said to him, so that you may dispose of me, of all that I am, with complete right and full liberty of loving, as one who feels himself perfectly loved. May you dispose of me, Word of God, (pardon the comparison) with the liberty with which you, while on earth, disposed of your most sacred humanity.

Yours so that, without asking me, without soliciting my consent, without taking me into the least account, you may dispose of my being and my life for the interior operations of your grace, for the exterior disposition of my life, for the immolation of my being.

It seemed to me that this practical, ardent donation, which made my soul and body tremble, was like a burning kiss that I impressed upon him, an immense, profound, ardent kiss in which my life and my being were breathed forth. I kissed him many times. Is not a kiss a sweet, swift contact of love in which the soul seems to escape into the breath?

I kissed him many times, meditating on that phrase in the Gospel: "She has not ceased to kiss my feet" (Luke 7:15). And it was precisely his feet that I was trying to kiss without stopping, believing myself unworthy of a more amorous kiss. But the daring desire of the spouse in the Canticle (1:1) was struggling within me to come forth and express itself. Père Lacordaire was so right. Love always has the same language, the same demands, the same stages.

At night, during another period of prayer, the roles were exchanged. Jesus, loving and compassionate, delivered himself to me. What ardor was his! What strength! What tenderness!

Can it be true, dear Master, that from your divine lips broke forth those words sweeter than honey! *I love you, I am yours,* and that meanwhile you united yourself to me and that you encompassed me with such divine ardor and energy that my weakness could scarcely support it?

In one of these periods of prayer—the first, I think—I felt the mysterious, irresistible attraction of Jesus; and I said to him: Who are you, mysterious Unknown, attracting me in this way, seizing me, stealing my soul so that my misery cannot withstand it, and almost causing me to lose my free will?

I also said to him: *My Tyrant of love!* Love is a sweet tyranny, and one who loves has no other language than that one, ever ancient and ever new, which in thousands of years has not lost its perennial freshness and which always has a never-fading youthfulness on the lips of one who loves.

Today the theme of yesterday continued, but more intense and firm. The *Yours* took great proportions, an unexpected amplitude; it seemed to eradicate all the barriers between Jesus and my soul, so that the sweet Beloved could now enter triumphantly into his garden of love.

The Beloved communicated himself without reserve to the soul of his loved one, like an impetuous torrent, with the pressure— pardon the word—of an infinite love. My soul sobbed with happiness under the weight of love and inflamed by superhuman love.

O Jesus, is it true that today you placed no other measure to your love than the indispensable measure of my smallness? I want you to love me like that. With divine liberty; I want you to pour yourself out without limit upon this poor little soul that belongs totally to you. It seems to me that you are avid to love in this way.

Even outside of prayer, the torrent of love continued pouring into the trench of my misery, as if it had been held back for many years. My soul tried to forsake itself, to abandon itself. When will it learn?

Several times I had to interrupt the Office because the gracious Tyrant of my soul shook it and made my body tremble with the floods of his impetuous, triumphant love.

An amiable mildness bathed my soul from dawn. Today all public worship ceased in the city;[5] everything in it is sadness and suffering. Why can I not dissemble my joy? It pains me, but what can I do? Can I be sad when love is celebrating its feast in my soul?

Joy is the perfume of love; and imbued with that perfume, I spent the day. He was with me and I with him, mysteriously communicating our love to each other. Those who love, find their universe in the magnificent isolation of their love; and today that universe was for me radiant with happiness. This lovely but fleeting isolation crowned a happy day.

Upon leaving Jesus for the night, in the ardor of my love I gently kissed the tabernacle curtain. Was it suggestion from my desire? Was it a blessed reality? God knows. I felt something like an electric shock, but *spiritual* and very delightful, which shook my whole being.

With my soul trembling and my body half swooning with love, I knelt at the foot of the altar, relishing the delight of what was, perhaps, a kiss from God.[6]

This was a delightful week, a week of love.[7] Impossible to describe my impressions. In prayer and even outside of it, I felt Jesus within me, but it seemed to me that he was no longer on the surface of my soul, as in preceding days, but in the bottom, far within, as if my heart had been opened to let him take possession of what belonged to him. My heart expanded gently and he filled it.

Sometimes I felt the indefinable, irresistible charm of the Beloved, like something delightful fastened in my heart, wounding it

[5] Public worship was suspended throughout the entire country from July 1, 1926, to June 29, 1929, because of the laws designed against the rights of the Church. But the legislature of Michoacán anticipated it, and worship in the State of Michoacán was suspended from April 18, 1926.

[6] Theologians call certain effects of divine contemplation infused into the will "divine touches or feelings," but they almost always have an overflow in the intellect. They are sometimes so profound that they seem to be impressed upon the substance of the soul. Then they are "substantial touches." The mystics speak of them as "God's embraces," or "divine kisses." But these touches are purely spiritual and supernatural; nothing of the sensible is to be seen here.

[7] From April 19 to 26, 1926.

as with a tender melancholy. That attraction drew me after Jesus irresistibly as if it might take me out of myself.

On Thursday, upon leaving Jesus, I perceived unmistakably that he was detaining me that I might make the Holy Hour near his tabernacle from eleven till twelve o'clock. Oh, the delight of that watch of love! The solemn solitude of the hour, the joy of having him detain me and the irresistible intimacy, familiarity, and affection noticeable in Jesus, filled this unforgettable hour with love and consolation. Even the fragrance of the lovely, fresh flowers which had been placed near my priedieu for him, spoke to me charmingly of love.

I cannot express nor shall I forget the heavenly impressions of this week of love.

Today I had to leave Mexico. When I said goodbye to Jesus, he seemed to be especially affable and affectionate toward me. With this impression, I entered the railway coach, disposed to give myself up freely to prayer and to love. I did so, in fact, for the space of one-half hour, because everything was favorable. I surrendered myself to God in deep recollection and with impetuous, sensible effusions of love. I felt myself united to God and I experienced a special joy in being alone with him without any obstacles. I was in a sort of somnambulistic state, as it were.

Little by little the impression that dominated in my spirit was joy that God was content; it pleased me that he could dispose of me without hindrance; no longer did I rejoice so much at being able to be with him freely all that afternoon, as much as that he could accomplish in my soul all he desired.

It seemed to me that his joy was my joy, that my own joy faded out before his joy and that I was happy precisely or principally because he was glad.

But, alas, this interior joy provoked a terrible tempest and a stormy period began. In vain did I take a harsh discipline right there in the train—twice, the tempest became so frightful.

The following day, in St. Clara's Church, I found peace in contemplating with tears and heartfelt tenderness the chasms of mercy in the heart of Jesus.

Some days of relative tranquillity passed. But eventually, the struggle was renewed in his soul.

The last tempest, illuminated by God's light, produced in me these ideas and resolutions: a deep knowledge of my wretchedness. I am always the same; all the remarkable graces of God which I have received of late have not changed my nothingness. Perhaps I need to be purified that the effusions of his love may continue in me and he has selected this painful purification.

I place myself in the divine hands, disposed for everything. I shall not get loose from them, come what may. I have an unalterable confidence in him. The immaculate Virgin Mary will be my support.

Afterwards the tempest returned; terrible and almost continuous until it suddenly ceased when the novena for Pentecost began.

God was preparing him for a special grace on the next feast of Pentecost.

On the fourteenth of May I commenced to be another person; all my passions were pacified and I again felt as formerly that the things of the world were very distant and that its fascinations scarcely touched me superficially. This peaceful state continued until the twenty-ninth of May, inclusive, my soul remaining united to God and touched by his love.

The grace for which the Bishop's soul was being prepared by trial was an oblation to the Holy Spirit on Pentecost. By the express will of God, as far as we can judge, he offered himself in a special manner to the Holy Spirit, making an oblation of his whole being and a consecration of his whole life. Moreover, he made a vow to extend the reign of the Holy Spirit as long as he lived and in all possible ways. All of this tended to unite him more to the "Works of the Cross."

On Pentecost with my whole soul I made the prescribed consecration and the vow for six months, for my spiritual director disposed it so for me.

Thus the novena as well as the octave of the Holy Spirit, but principally the latter, brought intimate union with the most holy Trinity. I modified my ordinary offering, which was directed only to the Father, and made it to the three divine Persons.

From May 31 to June 6 was a period of both struggle and consolation. Between May 31 and June 11 he merely states: "They were days of intense, ardent, delightful love, such as I had never experienced. It is better not to try to describe it."

From June 12 to June 19 love continued increasing until it became like an obsession. In his personal notes he writes of those days:

I remember especially two nights united by the charm of one loving emotion. A soul who has authentic communications with God assured me that he had told her he would receive great comfort in my oratory. Who can tell what I felt when this was told to me? For some moments I felt a kind of fainting with love. And then, even very far into the night, I relished this divinely delicious expression: *He is content.* But I wept, regretting that there was not room enough in my heart for all this heavenly sweetness.

Can the heart that loved ask for more? To think that he rejoices, that he is glad because of what I have prepared for him, happy with my company! I seemed to feel that night the nobility of love which forgets self to think only about the good of the beloved.

With my heart possessed by the welcome news, which I did not doubt because it was confirmed by something interior, I continued in this spirit the following days.

But on another night, in which I again prolonged my prayer, that experience impressed me under another aspect. I had begged Jesus to tell me if he loved me, through that urgency, that necessity, which one who loves feels of hearing from the beloved lips the unique word of love. And I thought, with the clarity which reason cannot give: if he is content here, it is because he loves me. The security of his love penetrated my whole being like a divine unction of joy. *He loves me! He loves me!* my soul repeated, quivering with emotion.

And half the night, before the tabernacle illuminated by the warm glow of the lamp, the eternal yet ever new dialog of love kept up between Jesus and my soul:

"Do you love me?"

"I love you. And you?"

"You know that I love You."

Dialog continually spoken yet never repeated!

These quotations suffice to give us some understanding of how our Lord was preparing the soul of Bishop Martínez for the grace of March 25, 1927. According to all indications, this grace was, as we said, that of the transforming union.

The foremost theologians agree that this union, although rare, is not on that account extraordinary or charismatic, like the gifts of prophecy, miracles, bilocations, stigmata and levitations. This union is the climax of the normal development of grace, of the virtues and the gifts; it is the prelude and the proximate preparation for the beatific union in heaven.

It would be an error to think that the transforming union is something sudden. On the contrary, preparation is made very far back; it progresses slowly. Even here is verified the adage, *nemo repente fit summus,* for no one reaches either the summit of good or the depths of evil suddenly.

Neither does this grace always conform to an invariable mold. All God's works display a rich variety, but also an admirable unity by reason of their source, their end and their very structure.

Finally, it must not be imagined that this union is ostentatious, exterior, sensible; on the contrary, it happens in the depth of the soul; therefore, it is most secret, hidden, interior; *it is all spiritual.*

Although we said that this grace is the normal peak of the development of grace, we must not think that it is therefore within *human* grasp. It is a gratuitous gift; God gives it to whom he wishes. Notwithstanding, the soul can and should prepare itself, removing obstacles, practicing the virtues, obeying the Holy Spirit with docility, and so on. And to one who does his part, it seems that God would not refuse this favor.

The transforming union consists essentially in a quasi-experimental knowledge of God and in the love that is born of such knowledge; it produces an almost constant union with God. It is a lofty, intellectual vision of God, the fruit especially of the gift of wisdom, through which the soul tastes and relishes how sweet is the Lord. Then the soul cannot doubt the presence of the three divine Persons within it, and it reaches the point where it almost never sees itself deprived of their company. It is a participation in the divine nature and life, the fullest and most perfect possible as far as the limitations of creatures permit, so that the soul feels that its union with God is definitive and inamissible.

Let us see how His Excellency speaks of this grace of March 25, 1927.

To whom but to you, Beloved of my soul, must I continue recounting the sweet story of our love? In this way, while writing, I shall think about you and love you; now that neither do you desire me to leave off loving you nor does my poor heart want to stop having that pleasure.

Do you remember, Jesus, that day of March 25, 1927? How you entered my soul? Without causing a disturbance, without making me feel even your sweetness, you arrived at this deep corner of my soul from which you have not departed and which I love, because you are there.[8]

Upon terminating that prayer, I had full security that I pos-

[8] His Excellency knew the technical terms of mystical theology. Nevertheless, it is noteworthy that here he forgets he is a theologian and speaks only as a mystic. And so what theologians call "the deepest center of the soul," he speaks of as the "deep recess," and the "sweet little corner." Here the three Persons dwell to unite themselves with the soul in a perfect and consummate union; and it is nothing else than the utmost limit that the nature of the soul, its virtue, the force of its operation and movement can attain; it is not possible to go farther. (Cf. St. John of the Cross, *Living Flame*, Stanza 1, verse 3.)

sessed you, the ineffable conviction that you were *mine,* and *mine* you will be for all eternity. Jesus, *mine, mine!*

The bases of this union, you know very well, were two: your mercy and my misery. Both are indestructible. You cannot stop being merciful nor can I stop being miserable.

How I thank you for letting me know that soon afterward—on the 28th—that what I had felt in my innermost soul was truth, sweet truth!

Do you remember my outbursts of jubilation, the deep impression of happiness that my soul could not hold? I thanked you and I tried to share the favor with other souls, for is not the best way of appreciating the possession of you to give you to others?

Since then, I carry you with me, you are mine; sometimes I feel you like a fire burning me; sometimes you burn sweetly in my innermost heart; sometimes my miseries cover me, tempests shake the surface of my soul, but within, in the blessed little corner, we are happy. You are happy, too, are you not?

How many things you have told me since you are living in my soul! Your way of speaking to me entrances me, and how well we understand each other! How many things you have done, too, in my soul!

On Good Friday you told me something. . . . Ah, Jesus, is it possible that my poor love takes that shade which embarrasses me, that you are going to fulfill that new, powerful desire of paternity surging up in my soul? What a mystery of love and of suffering began to unfold before my eyes!

Afterwards . . . how many things! Your union with me is inamissible and unalterable. I have already written what you made me understand about this (it was April 20).

In the ardor of your love you desired that we both be alone; we are better off that way. You permitted them to persecute me so you might take me entirely. Alone and only for you! Oh, sweet Love! What days we both have passed in this silence in which all the rejoicing of spring has been in harmony with the intimate canticle of our love. You know that I have been happy, very happy, and that at times this happiness does not fit into my heart.

Everyone pities me: they think that I am suffering greatly. They do not know that I am happy with your love and your companionship. Companionship? I do not like the word; it is suitable for earthly affections, not for this heavenly love. You are not living with me, you live *in me!*

How many years I yearned for love! May you be blessed for loving me just as I am; blessed for loving me with that love which exists only in your heart, so ardent, so tender, so delicate, so your very own! I cast myself definitively and without reservation into the ocean of that infinite love!

There had been days, one especially, on which I felt my misery very deeply; it seemed to me, that day at least, that the consciousness of my imperfections obscured the happiness of my love. But you know how to convert all bitterness into sweetness with the divine alchemy of your love.

You told me that my wretchedness enamored you. What taste you have! . . . Your interior light has raised the veil of the mystery a little, my Beloved, and I desire to be infinite nothingness rather than annihilate myself through love.

While reading St. Thérèse of the Child Jesus—now see how much you have taught me; you gave her to me as teacher—it occurred to me that if you raised her in your arms because she thought her soul so small, my soul is also small, not with the charming littleness of the child, but with the repelling weakness of the infirm.

But you are the Good Samaritan who cures the wounds of my soul and finishes up by uniting yourself to it with immense love. But you have either surpassed the parable of the Good Samaritan or you have discovered to me its profound meaning. Jesus, you cure my miseries with kisses of love and you do not place me upon a beast, but within your heart.

The day that I felt my misery most keenly, you gave me to know your mercy. For such deep misery an infinite mercy was necessary!

What you have done with me, you probably have not done to anyone else. I am a monument to your mercy.

And since you said with your divine lips that one who has been pardoned much ought to love much, I ought to love you with an exceptional love, perhaps as no one else, because you have had mercy on me as on no one else. I am disposed to fulfill that duty of loving you much, of loving you in an exceptional way; if you grant me that love, your enamored Magdalen is going to remain behind.

Pardon my ravings, my Master, but why not tell you in writing what you are reading in my soul?

In *The Story of a Soul,* I read these words: "I feel that if, however impossible, you might find a soul weaker than mine, you would take pleasure in loading her with still greater favors, provided that she abandoned herself with full confidence to your infinite mercy!" Then I thought that my soul is unquestionably weaker than that of St. Thérèse. Oh, if I might know my weakness and abandon myself entirely to your infinite mercy!

But no; I do not wish to receive either more or fewer gifts than those you have given to another soul; I want only to please you; I want what you want.

May 4. Solemnity of St. Joseph.

I commenced to love you in a new way, my Jesus; my love took on an intense, sweet tone. It gives me shame and joy at the same time to tell it to you. I began to love you as something *my own;* but not like something of mine that I possess, but like *mine that I am.* Pardon my boldness, I began to love you like a prolongation of my being, as mothers must love their children. Did not St. Joseph love you in this way? That blessed saint made me participate in his love. What a special love this is! One loves in a different way when the Beloved is not yet ours. . . . Oh, *mine!*

May 6. First Friday.

You completed the grace. You told me—why should I not say "You told me,"[9] since you have a gentle manner of speaking without out words?—you told me that to *that* way of loving you as *mine,*

[9] Neither "distinct contemplation" nor "locutions" are discussed here, but "indistinct contemplation" in which God, without locutions, makes the soul understand what he desires.

corresponds a way of loving me as *yours,* but the *yours* understood as the *mine,* that is, not as a thing possessed, but as a prolongation of the being.

It is clear that this is the mystical union of love.[10]

You revealed your secret to me. First, you take possession of the beloved little corner; for that I must give you all my affection. But you do not simply remain there and nothing more; you keep on extending yourself, invading my entire being, transforming it into you: heart, soul, character, body, all. Little by little you live more in me; a day will come on which you may speak by my mouth, work by my actions, suffer in my sorrows, and love through my heart; a day will come on which we may be one single thing.[11]

No longer will those poor terms *mine, yours,* suffice us, will they? We shall substitute for *you, I,* (that is to say, I transformed into you.) When will that be, my Jesus? We both desire it so ardently! Ah, by dint of caresses and kisses of love, you must destroy my miseries and my obstacles to union. Well, Jesus, heal me, for that medicine is delicious, and when I am well, follow me in the same way, treating me until I am sick with love.

I have offered and given my whole being to you, piece by piece, so that you may take it, possess it, and live in me and transform me into you. It matters little that you desire me so as to immolate me. Happy immolation by the Priest, Love.[12]

[10] In the exposition of this grace, His Excellency, without endeavoring to do so, points out the characteristics or effects of the transforming union: certainty of the possession of God, the continuation of the divine presence, the consciousness that such possession is definitive and inammisible, the full communication of the divine life, etc. Regarding the inamissibility of this union, it should be observed that theologians are accustomed to point out, among the effects of the transforming union, the certainty of salvation. But since the Council of Trent defined that no one can be absolutely certain of his salvation without a divine revelation, some theologians think that the transforming union is equivalent to that revelation; others think it suffices for that certainty that the virtue of hope be especially confirmed.

[11] A perfect description of the transforming union.

[12] Reference is made to the expression in the liturgy: *Amor sacerdos immolat,* for love is the priest that immolates Jesus.

Jesus, you asked me to love you greatly, that I do nothing else than love you. You told me that you had an immense thirst for love and you said to the Samaritan woman, "Give me to drink."

You know, O my thirsting Master, that yesterday and today I gave you all the scant water of love that my poor heart contains. Drink, Jesus, drink what is yours! Drink all the love of my heart; I should like you to be satisfied and yet I should not like it! That you be satisfied so as to quench your desires; and that you should not be satisfied, so that you may always be asking me for a drink, and I always giving it to you.

O Jesus, you know that I love you and you know how I should like to love you. You know the immense happiness that it is for my soul to give you to drink; because I do not want to think about myself. To give you pleasure, my Beloved, is my supreme happiness, my only happiness! To give you pleasure always, to give you pleasure in everything! This is felicity; this is heaven.

I do not even dare to ask you to take away those miseries that make me suffer so greatly. If you wish me to endure them, I shall be happy to endure them. I wish to ask you for nothing; I need nothing. It is enough for me that you are content, that you are happy, that I am giving you pleasure.

I desire what you desire in the sufferings of my country; I adore and I love your loving designs upon my soul and upon the souls whom I love.

O Jesus! O Beloved! O my own!

From May 13 to May 31 our Lord instructed His Excellency as we have described, without words, without locutions, but with an interior illumination.

Look, Jesus, when you want to give souls a lesson, you hide yourself well. You are not going to reveal the slightest trace of your beauty, because the lesson would fail and be converted into an idyl. This happened now in my soul. I commenced my prayer wishing only to please you. What do you want of me?, I said to you; how can I please you during these moments?

He considered himself incapable of providing any pleasure

to our Lord; but the interior answer came at once: "One thing: to come down, uniting myself to your soul."

Of course! You are the Word annihilated; and since you humbled yourself when you came into this world, a passionate taste for descending has remained with you. Descend then, divine Word, for giving you pleasure gives me happiness.

And you began to give me a lesson: inasmuch as I have surrendered myself to you, and since we are going to live together, I must mold myself to your taste. Yours must be mine.

And I began to relish that pleasure of being forgotten, that no one take notice of me, that they humiliate me.

He wished to follow our Lord on the way of his abasement, but suddenly, like a flash of heavenly light, he caught a glimpse of his beauty.

Ah! Everything about you is beautiful, even what seems insignificant; but that loving abasement, O Word annihilated, has an incomparable beauty!

I do not attempt to analyze it, because beauty cannot be analyzed, one enjoys it and receives its irresistible influence. And although another beauty might be analyzed, yours, which I saw today, withstands all analysis. I do not know what I say; I only know that my heart burned and that since that moment I could not help but love you with ardor, with passion.

"Did we not feel our hearts burn when he was talking to us in the way?" asked the disciples of Emmaus. When Jesus reveals himself a little,—what shall I say?—when he approaches, although it may be half-veiled, hearts burn.

Now I understand why you are the 'hidden God' and why you are veiled with the shadows of faith. If you were to appear unveiled, hearts would burn up, the world would be dazed, normal life would be impossible.

What a Son you have, O Virgin Mary! He carefully hides his beauty to avoid catastrophes. And he hides everything, everything, because everything in him is beautiful and desirable, even the most trifling characteristic, even the least movement.

O Virgin Mary, carefully hide your Son, if you do not want the world to catch fire.

Perhaps there is no more efficacious means of teaching than love. With that method I believe that I shall learn all you teach me.

You have constituted yourself my teacher of love, and with such a teacher I shall progress rapidly in that divine science, in spite of my dullness. During these days you have given me magnificent lessons:

To love is to give you pleasure in everything, to have no other will than yours, to love your will passionately and adore it submissively, and to do all this with delicacy, with courtesy, putting as much love in the manner as in the substance.

But today's lesson pleased me greatly; I shall not forget it and I shall always practice it. You taught me our mutual rights. It is evident that love has its rights and very well established ones. Since love has made me yours, you have full right over what was mine before; over the most intimate thoughts of my soul, over my words and actions, over every breath, and over every heart-beat; you have rights over every instant of my life and *especially over the details of my death*. O Jesus, what a delight to be yours!

But you taught me today that I have rights over you. You are mine! Of course I have the right of disposing of my own. Disposing of you is to know you and to love you; I have then the right to contemplate you when I wish, the right to gaze upon you to my satisfaction.

And during this afternoon, you made me exercise this right. Although hidden under so many veils, I discerned your mysterious beauty, O divine Word, and my poor soul did not tire of gazing upon you, as the one who thirsts does not tire drinking the crystal waters. Your beauty seizes the soul, enkindles the heart; the one who looks at you surrenders himself to you without reserve.

I learned, then, that I am the more yours, as you are the more mine.

But what fills me and distracts me is the right of looking at you. It is very natural to have that right: how could I not have the right of looking at my own? But in the depths of my soul is the certainty you gave me that I have that right. Would that I could never take my eyes off your beauty!

The lesson ended in gratitude. How much I thank you for having loved me! How much I thank you for letting me look at you!

The Divine Master's pedagogy, according to Archbishop Martínez, does not proceed step by step like that of earthly teachers; it flies. This is natural, for love does not walk, it flies. Perhaps for that reason the Holy Spirit appeared in the form of a dove. Still more, since love is fire, it has its own rapid way of spreading.

Our Lord prepared His Excellency for this lesson with a truly terrible temptation. It was a tremendous struggle in which only at the cost of heroic efforts did his soul come out victorious, but humbled. When calm was restored, his soul was prepared to receive this delightful lesson in love.

You want me to love you always, at every instant! You have full right to demand it, since I am all yours. With what tenderness and ardor you asked it of me! These are lessons in love, given by love and with immense love.

Your petition touched my soul. One does not ask for love except when one loves. One does not ask for love at every instant except when one is desperately in love.

O Jesus, ask me for love, ask me for great love, so I may feel the happiness of seeing you enamored of my wretchedness! To love you without ceasing is for me a daydream, happiness; but it is impossible to realize this happiness if you do not teach me, if your Holy Spirit does not put that love into me.

To do nothing else but love you means to give you pleasure always and with extreme delicacy—forgetting myself and thinking about you—to consecrate to you without reserve every beating of my poor heart.

Desiring to put into practice your sublime lesson, I understood that I need, in order *to love you always, to sacrifice myself without ceasing.*

It cost me great effort to understand today's lesson. It seemed to me that you wanted me to look at you; but my poor gaze was lost in the shadows that envelop your beauty. No doubt your light shines in the midst of the shadows, but who can perceive it if the Holy Spirit does not give him to know it?

But more than words, you gave me the key with an objective lesson: "Look at me with love!", you wanted to say to me. And looking at you that way, my eyes found you. Love's eyes are quick in discovering the beloved, in becoming acquainted with him. Just as things are taught to a child, you began to teach me to look at you with love. I understood that I was lacking the simplicity needed to understand your lessons. O my Jesus, each lesson of yours is not only an instruction, but a divine stimulus to love. Love is taught by loving.

Therefore, do you want me to direct toward you glances of love? You would not ask me for those looks if you did not love me. Now I see it all clearly: since you want me to love you always, at other times I shall love you by working or suffering for your love; but in these delightful moments of intimacy, what is more natural than to love you by looking at you, directing toward you glances of love? That is the way lovers do.

What is a look of love? Is it love that goes through the eyes or the soul seeking in the Beloved the sweet incentive of love? A look of love, is it surrender or possession? When one looks, is love expressed or is it asked for? Who can explain the mystery of a look of love?

Looking at Jesus, I possess him; because he is light, and light is taken possession of by the look. But my soul is in the light of my eyes, too; my love is here to be immersed in light. But, most sweet Master, the look of perfect love needs to meet another look; when will you grant my eyes to meet the light of your look? Just as a giddy child tries in his stupid way to put a lesson into practice, I have stupidly attempted looks of love.

Today's lesson did not have the charm of other lessons, but its teachings were very profound.

Last night I suddenly felt the charm, the delight of having everyone forget me, of having no one occupied with me, so as to belong completely to you, my Master, to be only for you, so that we may be alone. And in the morning you wanted to confirm that sweet impression in my soul.

Today, your lesson began with the theme: *We two alone!* You want my soul to live alone with you in the immense, magnificent solitude of love. You told me to what a point your jealous love wants me to be yours. You had told me this before, but your words never really penetrated.

You desire me to think only about you, love only you, hope only in you and depend only on you. How it pleases me for you to ask me that! I understand how much you love me.

You made me see by how many chains I am still bound to creatures and how much there is in me that is not totally yours. You know that I understand love as total surrender and that affectively I have made it to completion. It is now your turn to help my weakness so that it may be perfect *effectively* in my life.

Permit me a comparison to tell you how I understand what you are asking of me. As a wife gives herself up completely to her husband, so that she wishes only what he wishes; so that only from him does she expect the necessities of life; so that she does not wish to do anything except the will of her spouse, although he might want to renounce her; for she wishes to take what falls to her lot, but, more, still more. . . . Words cannot explain what I understand.

Well then, I want to be yours, O Jesus! You know what you are doing in me interiorly and exteriorly. You are my only Master and my only possession. Only we two! *You and I!* Behold my universe, my all! Like St. Thérèse of the Child Jesus, I wish that all creatures be nothingness for me and I nothingness for all creatures.

How deep, how refreshing, how difficult the solitude of love! Naturally, you will be mine in the measure in which I am yours. Only for me! It seems to me that today we made the mutual promise of this perfect, loving solitude. When will it be realized?

Archbishop Martínez had excellent teachers, but none like Christ, for it is written: "Blessed is the man whom thou hast taught" (Ps. 98:12).

You showed your immense love toward me, that jealous love which is satisfied only with the full possession of my entire being. Although I felt the happiness of being loved, it seemed to me that such happiness should be eclipsed in the presence of the joy of satisfying you, of surrendering myself to your love.

To let oneself love is a delight; but for that an absolute solitude is necessary. You want to love me alone; I also wish to love you that way, nothing standing in the way of your divine communications, with nothing hindering my complete giving.

I want to be alone with you, despoiled of everything, *consecrated only to you.* Whatever you wish, I also wish. You see the sincerity of my heart and also my misery. You, for you are powerful, make my solitude perfect; draw from me everything created to cast me totally into you, although for this I may have to sacrifice myself. Tell me what I ought to do.

And you said to me very gently: *"Give me pleasure in everything."*

Ah, I do, indeed, live for that, I exist to give you pleasure! What happiness to please you always, to live for that! When you indicate to me your pleasure, to fulfill it without hesitating, expeditiously, tenderly, delicately, forgetful of my happiness and thinking about yours. When you do not let me know your pleasure, to guess it, always with disinterestedness and delicacy. In this way to change everything into love.

O Jesus, what a beautiful lesson! That is to love, to be loved alone; that is to be happy and (as they say in the world and properly qualifying this expression when applied to you), to make you happy.

Creatures? One can go to God through them or, rather, find God in them and there be alone with God. O Jesus, Jesus, teach me to love in this way, show me how we may love each other alone!

Today's lesson was fitting conclusion to this heavenly treatise on love.

I do not know how you taught me that *you desire to do everything in me.* Not only because my misery requires you to desire this, but through excess of love—why explain it?—and upon making me understand this excess of yours, you let me see that all my obligations of love, or rather, their basis is as St. Thérèse of Lisieux said: *gratitude* and *abandonment*.

To let oneself be loved is to love in a delicate, intense way; it is something very pleasing to you and very sweet to me.

All afternoon I was transported with loving emotion and at night I could not sleep.

I shall not forget, O Jesus, the house full of flowers and of songs where we both spent the lovely spring; especially that little corner.[13] But it is always spring with you and everywhere it is heaven.

On the 30th, the eyes of my spirit seemed to be transfixed in you, without my being able to take them away. On the 31st, a great love united me with you. Do you remember that in my loving eagerness I asked you persistently to unite finally yourself with me definitively and to tell me the obstacle which opposes the communication of our love? You answered me very soon.

Our Lord gave Bishop Martínez to understand that on the next feast of Pentecost he might renew his vow of purity in the sense peculiar to the Congregation of the Missionaries of the Holy Spirit, that this vow would be like a special bond with that Congregation and, finally, that he would attain the full glow and strength of that virtue.

Note well that *purity* does not precisely signify *chastity;* the latter is something very elementary, proper rather to beginners. It treats of purity in its whole extension: *negatively,* it is the

[13] On account of the religious persecution, His Excellency was hidden, first, in the Motherhouse of the Little Sisters of the Poor; it was very spacious, with garden, orchard, flowers, birds. It had previously been the summer home of the Archbishop of Morelia, who gave it to these religious. There Bishop Martínez received all these graces. A short time afterwards, the house was informed against, the religious were thrown into the street, and the house transferred to the informer. His Excellency was then hidden in a downtown house which for some time had been empty. The secret of this hiding place was kept with such vigilance that no one, except four intimate persons, knew about it.

absolute detachment from all creatures and from one's self; *positively,* it is the abundance of grace that divinizes the soul; it is an emptiness of creatures and a plenitude of God; it is not only a virtue but a gift of the Holy Spirit.

In this sense, the more pure a soul, the more it is united with God; or it may be that the degrees of union are measured by the degrees of purity. Therefore, it is very natural that our Lord should ask His Excellency for more purity in order to be more intimately united with him.

To love God with the *whole* heart is to be very pure; in other words, purity and love are like the opposite sides of the same cloth. To be pure is to be unworldly. To be perfectly pure is to be completely unworldly; and to be completely unworldly is to love God totally; it is to be filled with him.

On the other hand, God is infinite purity. Each one of the divine Persons has, so to speak, his own shade of purity. For a soul to be united with infinite purity it must be participated purity. And the union itself of both purities has to be a mystery of purity.

Today, Pentecost, I made my renovation in this form: "For the glory of the august Trinity, to honor especially the Holy Spirit and under his aid and protection, in the hands of Mary Immaculate, I renew, confirm and affirm my vow of purity with the intention and the desire of embracing all the glow and the strength of that virtue, and of binding my union with the Works of the Cross and especially with the Congregation of the Missionaries of the Holy Spirit.

"I beg the Holy Spirit in a very special way, through the hands of Mary Immaculate, to grant me all the graces that I need to fulfill what I promise and to obtain what only he can bestow upon me."

My supplication had been heard by you, O Jesus, and full of kindness you told me what was necessary to make our union firm.

CHAPTER V

Crowning Grace

THE ENTIRE OCTAVE of that Pentecost was steeped, as it were, in purity. Bishop Martínez had begged the Holy Spirit for purity in order to resemble Jesus and to realize the Father's ideal. It seemed to him that when our Lord asked him to renew his vow of purity on Pentecost, he was demanding a more exquisite care in fleeing even from what is less pure, as well as more love and eagerness for purity. But, at the same time, he understood that in that petition, through our Lord's delicacy, a promise was enclosed, the promise of making him more pure; for, "the whole strength of purity"[1] is not the fruit of the virtue, but of the gifts of the Holy Spirit.

But that gift could not come without a struggle. From June 12 to June 15 a terrible tempest raged, a tempest of the spirit, a tempest of the passions, in which the devil played a special part. In the midst of the tremendous struggle, Jesus was his strength. Many times he felt separated from him, but upon kneeling before the tabernacle, he found our Lord full of tenderness and of mercy, as always. Many times Christ himself calmed his agitation and restored peace to his soul.

But even in the midst of the combat, the lessons of the divine Master were not interrupted. He made him see the difficulty of sincerity even with ourselves, with what facility we can deceive ourselves. It seemed to His Excellency that if we can be deceived in everything, the spirit can with difficulty establish itself upon solid ground. But when he approached the tabernacle, our

[1] "Vigor totius puritatis," *Roman Pontifical*.

Lord gave him an understanding of faith. Through faith our spirit can be established upon the rock of certainty.

When in the midst of the storm the sky appears, it seems clearer than before. The sun shines and its rays are like sparkles of hope placed in the blackness of the tempest. So, in the midst of my struggles you appeared, O Jesus; kindly, like a pledge of peace.

Little by little, too slowly, the storm subsided; but you were illuminating the heaven of my soul more rapidly with your immortal light.

You were teaching me that you have regard for all the aspirations of my soul; that all my desires, apparently multiple, are basically desires for you. My desires were simplified in the single desire for you. But one feels this without being able to explain it. I saw my soul like an immense need for Jesus, like an immense capacity for Jesus, like an immense thirst for Jesus.

I saw a wonderful harmony between you and me; between your riches and my misery; between your greatness and my smallness. Just as when an orange is separated, the sections of one-half fit the sections of the other, so that a projection on one part corresponds to a hollow on the other; so it seems to me that you and I fit marvelously; but in our case all the hollow is on my side and all the plenitude on yours.

Only you suffice for me, O Jesus! You are my all. You satisfy all the noble, legitimate aspirations of my soul, from those that look to my own interests to the most disinterested desires of my heart; you are the desired one, the only one of my soul. In your love are all the shades of love that the heart of man can ambition!

To divest oneself of everything so as to be filled with God, so that he may be the *All* of the soul, such is true purity.

About a year and a half before, His Excellency had written: "Each day I perceive better, sometimes sensibly, the attraction of purity. Purity is indispensable for love; it might be said that they are the obverse and the reverse of the same reality. To draw near to God, *to look at him,* to love him, one must be pure, very pure. Degrees of light and of love correspond to the degrees of purity. What happiness to feel clean, to feel free and to leave earth's sadness so as to immerse oneself in God."

Years later he wrote: "I ought to take exquisite care to keep my soul perfectly pure, enveloped in purity, so that God may unite himself to it, and so as not to hinder that loving unbosoming of divine tenderness.[2]

"Formerly God made me understand that my soul needs to be very pure to be able to deal holily with the many pure souls that he has entrusted to me. But afterwards he made me see that I need still greater purity to deal with God, to receive his 'touches' which are my life. These divine contacts purify; but the purer the soul, the purer and the more intense the union."

Some time afterwards, in a letter to a close friend, His Excellency said:

You cannot imagine the impression produced upon me by what you say in your August letter about the impression of purity that contact with my soul produces upon you. Before you, another soul had told me the same. Moreover, upon taking leave of the Delegate, September 24, to go to Querétaro, he said to me: "Since you scatter blessings wherever you go, leave a very copious one for Bishop Banegas."[3]

Both impressions are closely connected; and the light of God, like a lightning flash, made me see what I prefer not to see, what embarrasses me: that there is truth in what is said, that our Lord has accomplished a marvelous work in me.

In the brightness of that flash, I felt a strange impression: *holy* satisfaction, but more, much more, shame and embarrassment. I do not want to see *that* nor do I explain it to myself. To flee from the shame I took refuge in my miseries; with them I feel at ease, in peace, in my own circle. My remedy is to close my eyes to what is within and to open them to look at my poor tatters. But how to reconcile the strange revelation with the indisputable reality of my miseries?

[2] The Archbishop refers here to what the mystics call "divine touches."
[3] At the time, Bishop Banegas was seriously ill.

On the awards day at the seminary, when I gave Benediction, I saw the solution of the problem: I had the monstrance in my hands; the sacred host was near my eyes; and my soul was filled with light. Within me is infinite purity and the supreme benediction; how could I help but diffuse around me purity and blessings? But that heavenly treasure is hidden in a coat of miseries, and, blessed be God that it is so! Those blessed miseries cover with a veil the divine that would dazzle me. I could not live without them, because they are the peace of my life, my magnet for attracting the Lord; they make it possible to live on earth carrying in my soul the life of God.

In his private notes he also wrote:

I have had many other lights during this season: Jesus needs to be *understood* because all who love, experience this imperious need. During his mortal life, he passed through the world without being understood. Only Mary and, in a certain measure, St. Joseph and perhaps St. John understood him. In his mystical life, how few souls comprehend him! How few understand his tastes, divine his desires, fathom his words!

This matter of comprehending Jesus is a new stage of intimacy and proceeds from purity in all its forms. To understand him, one needs recollection, which is purity from exterior things; the purity that consists in freedom from the influence of the passions; purity of heart that includes the emptying of all human affection and the perfection of divine love; and purity of understanding to comprehend the divine language: "Blessed are the clean of heart for they shall see God."

How much purity the Lord demands of me in all my actions, affections and intentions! True delicacies which, without doubt, will help toward perfect intimacy.

Quotations could be multiplied, but these suffice to make us realize what I said at the beginning—that purity was one of the characteristic features of the interior life of Archbishop Martínez.

This brings us to the discussion of another characteristic trait of the Archbishop's spirituality, his humility. This humility is of the style of St. Thérèse of Lisieux, it is the humility of smallness, proper to "spiritual infancy"; the humility that formed the essence of what His Excellency called "the mystery of weakness"; the humility that consists not only in recognizing our misery, but in coming to love it; the humility that makes us submerge ourselves joyously in our nothingness, *the humility of annihilation.*

The Archbishop's whole ideal was to attain that supreme strength, that invincible energy which is love, more powerful than death, as powerful as God, for it conquers his divine heart. And the road that he followed, the infallible way to reach it, was his own weakness, recognized and loved. Therefore he selected as his motto: *Cum infirmor, tunc potens sum.* He found the secret of his strength in his weakness. As he wrote in his personal notes:

My life is composed of something divine which Jesus pours out profusely in me—*light, union, love*—and a veil of misery with which he guards his treasure. I love the treasure which I bear within because it is his, because it is he; but I also love the veil that guards it. Who does not know that on earth it is necessary to guard treasures? Only in heaven are they exhibited in the light of glory. The veil does not hinder me from increasing my treasure and enjoying it; but, how could I stop loving the veil that guards it?

Misery is not only the guardian of humility and interior detachment is not only the magnet that attracts the Beloved; they are both a reminder of him, because when he lived on earth, he bore our miseries upon himself. I think that from heaven he must love his fatigue, his sleep, his agony and his tears.

Our poor limitations are like a copy of the blessed remembrance; they resemble that earthly veil which covered the beauty of Jesus for thirty-three years, and that other veil, mysterious and so very white, which hides his divine charms in the tabernacle.

Doubtless, all limitations in Christ were most pure and even our iniquities, which God placed upon him, did not stain him; rather, they were expiated and destroyed by his triumphant purity. Alas, our miseries have such close relationships with sin! But I do not love them for those low connections. I love them because in contact with the divine light they are changed into the brightness of truth; I love them because they hide from the gaze of all, even my own, the dazzling treasure that makes one blush; I love them because they remind me of the dear veil in which the Beloved was wrapped during his mortal life and of the veil that guards his Eucharistic life.

Of my miseries, what shall I say? That I love them, that I do not want to live without them. St. Francis of Assisi was enamored of "Lady Poverty" and through her he went to Jesus, poor, crucified and burning with love. It seems to me that I am enamored of "Lady Misery" and that through her I must penetrate that heart filled with sorrow and inflamed with love.

I think that the poverty St. Francis loved was not only the exterior, which all understand, but also the complete poverty, especially spiritual, for the rags of wretchedness join the soul with perfect poverty in such a way that Jesus, who so loved poverty, must unite himself with the soul that is dressed in it.

In spite of the usual claim that the contemplation of our wretchedness disturbs confidence, I defend the fondness I have for my rags, because I judge them irreproachable; to me they even seem a matter of good taste. Although I might belong to all the aristocracies, how deny my native misery? Bishop and saint I might be, I am a poor little thing lacking all spiritual goods, whom love has elevated. Why forget what I was and what I continue being, seeing that "the monkey, although dressed in silk, remains a monkey"?

To think about my rags has the charm of truth and of justice and it is by no means an obstacle to appreciating and even adding luster to God's graces. But it has another secret charm, the ineffable charm that the origin of his love has for the lover, the lure with which it attracted the heart of the Beloved. Are not our miseries, our rags, the things that captivated the divine lover? And are not

they or their remembrance what continues attracting and imprison-
ing the beloved heart?

Pardon the word—it is not lack of respect, it is that we have
only human words to speak of the divine—but for one who knows
Jesus, it is very fine *coquetry* to love the old rags and even the new
ones that we wear under the aristocratic garments that we received
from him. Aside from this, my affection is instinctive and sweet;
each one is as he is.

On the other hand, the desire that Jesus will not reveal himself
to me, the inability to withstand his beauty, is not owing to my
unworthiness and smallness; neither is it through lack of confidence; it is the tint of my love, it is an excess of sensibility—although in everything else I may have slight sensibility. I marvel at
Mary most holy, who lived thirty-three years with Jesus without
veils to cover him or her eyes; I marvel at the souls that on earth
live, as it were, in heaven and have the strength to gaze upon the
splendor of the Beloved and to submerge themselves in the ocean
of his unspeakable caresses.

But I cannot imitate those prodigies; I live happily, guessing at
the sovereign beauty behind a veil, discreet and mysterious, and
breathing the mild fragrance of the Beloved in the slight trace
which he leaves wherever he passes by triumphantly. Neither my
spirit nor my heart nor my flesh may support more, and I do not
think that I receive less than strong souls, but that I receive it in
another way.

Jesus is my repose: in the midst of my activity and my sufferings, I need interior, complete rest; I find it in Jesus. At night,
especially, when I enter my chapel—poorer and smaller than the
last one, but more personal and perhaps more dear—I throw myself into the heart of my All, and I forget the burden of the day,
and I feel recompensed for my labor and suffering in the peaceful,
complete, loving repose in my Jesus. May he also rest in me!
Where must Allness rest if not in nothingness, but in a nothingness full of love?

After His Excellency had preached a sermon in Salvatierra

on our Lady of Light, a priest, a sincere friend of his, remarked to him that he praised God through the talent he had given him. The prelate wrote:

I did not receive this favorably, for I had told Jesus that day that I want no talent, virtue or ability other than himself. It satisfies me to be a nothingness for Jesus to fill.

Ah, if these graces of God and these praises of men want to exalt me, the miseries that oppress me would be enough to drag me along the ground. Blessed miseries! Blessed my rags that make me capable of receiving the gifts of God! Let no one try to take them away, because I shall never let them go. Now I am convinced that these miseries will never be taken away from me and I remain calm, for on the surface there is a storm and in the bottom, pearls; outside, tatters and inside, Jesus.

We insist that it is necessary to determine precisely or to rectify the concept of *miseries!* Those treated of here frequently do not have even an imperfection; they are humiliating, but they do not offend our Lord. We shall understand them only with difficulty, if we do not have the light of self-knowledge of holy souls, the delicacy of their conscience, or the refinement of their love.

A very slight discord, an almost imperceptible lack of tuning, is nothing for unfamiliar ears; but for a great artist it is insupportable. Something like this happens with these miseries; ordinary, simple good souls do not even notice them; but how much they make holy souls suffer!

Nevertheless, His Excellency came to understand that there is something better than to recognize and love one's own misery, and that is not to take it into account at all. For to rivet attention on one's own wretchedness, even when it is to recognize it and to accept it, is still to have the mind on oneself. Perfect humility is *forgetfulness of oneself,* because it is the *death of the ego.*

The key of my life is in this, that I disappear completely and that God may do everything in me. Without doubt, I have always seen this and thought about it; but now I see it in a *new* way. That new way which God wishes me to enter, according to the lights of the feast of the Sacred Heart, is precisely a deeper disappearance of myself and a new and perfect way of God's possessing me, ruling me and working in me.

I perceive it, but I still do not come near understanding it exactly, much less explaining it. I must lose all self-confidence, my whole will and all my tastes, and permit myself to be guided and formed by God in my life and in my activity. If these designs of God are realized, how much he will do for me! How much he will do in me!

I made a curious contract with Jesus, with the following clauses, more or less:

1) Convinced that I must always have miseries, and that I cannot take them away, and that if duly supported they are stairs to go to God; knowing moreover that I am losing time—which I should occupy in something better—looking at these miseries; I bind myself not to look at them deliberately.

2) Keeping the eyes of my soul free in virtue of the preceding clause, I dedicate them to looking at Jesus always and in everything, so far as my frailty permits; and in the same way, keeping my heart free from anxieties about myself, I shall be consecrated entirely to him.

3) Jesus, on his part, bound himself to look upon my miseries to take away those that displease him and to utilize those that please him.

4) Jesus bound himself also to look at me with that look of love which illuminates and cleanses souls, embellishes them, sanctifies and makes them happy.

In view of the extraordinary humility and purity that our Lord bestowed upon Archbishop Martínez, it is not strange that he elevated him to such a close union. Let us see the final preparations for the crowning grace of September 21, 1927.

Around the feast of the Sacred Heart, I saw how that heart is made for mine, that is to say, how both correspond; my heart full of miseries, that heart full of mercy; my heart, craving to be loved, that heart, loving infinitely; my heart, never sated with loving, that heart, inexhaustibly lovable.

The other day I saw clearly that my heart ought to be separated from everything so as to be concentrated on Jesus, that I ought to sacrifice all my affections to his victorious love.

To tear the heart from everything created is to be pure; and then to give it to Jesus, is to love.

Jesus satisfies all the aspirations of my soul, all the tones of affection for which my heart longs. Jesus is my all. When will my heart be perfectly simplified in him?

On the feast of the Sacred Heart I made my offering as victim of Merciful Love, according to the formula and the spirit of St. Thérèse of the Child Jesus.

I had struggles and temptations; I became more deeply aware of my misery than ever; I saw that I had never been sufficiently buried in my nothingness. Formerly I saw that I was miserable, but I saw *something;* now I understand a little that I am *nothing.*

I seemed to stand before Jesus, sick, powerless, covered with tatters and as if I were a criminal, deserving of contempt and horror. Full of shame I threw myself into the bosom of love; unworthy of being in Jesus' presence, I aspired to his love through a necessity that seemed almost out of place.

But, ah, there is a wonderful affinity between us. His infinite mercy corresponds to my immense miseries. That his mercy is infinite means that neither our miseries nor our sins exhaust it.

He is infinite in pardoning just as I am immense in my malice; he is eager to cleanse, to repair, just as I am full of failings and of stains; he is immense in power, just as I am absolutely powerless and he loves this wretchedness, this nothingness, this impotence, with a passionate love. He lowers himself even to the immensity of my nothingness with the immensity of his love. He is my strength, my purity, my all.

Rightly did St. Thérèse of the Child Jesus say that the way to love is abandonment. To reach love *Nothingness* must abandon itself to *Allness*.

I have profited greatly from what God inspires me to say to souls. As the secretary of a very wise man learns from the letters and writings which he dictates, so I learn from what God says to souls through my unworthy person.

One of the things that I learned was how Jesus is a "hidden God." Everything in him is hidden: the foundation of his doctrine, of his morality, of the Christian life. The world does not understand him.

The most lovable and the beautiful aspect of Jesus, is the hidden, the mysterious. Jesus pleases me that way, he enamors me, *hidden*.

If my poor intellect could exhaust his beauty and his charms, if my poor heart could exhaust his love, Jesus would not fill me, for I being nothingness, only the infinite fills me, he would not be Jesus.

Whatever in Jesus exceeds my thought, surpasses my desires, and escapes my affections, whatever is hidden in him, the mysterious, this is what distracts me, what agitates me.

To find its hidden Beloved, the soul must be hidden also: through purity it is hidden from creatures, through humility it is hidden from itself, through recollection it is hidden from everything. And through love it is hidden in the bosom of its Beloved to enjoy the *hiddenness;* the inebriating and eternal hiddenness of its Beloved.

The fear of a physical suffering, genuine but made greater by my imagination, helped my soul greatly. Jesus makes use of simple things to do us good. It gave me pleasure to accept for him all that might come and not even to ask him—in spite of my vacillations—to diminish the pain or the consequences. He treated me with such tenderness, he surrounded me with such comforts like a mother indulging her child, as if he should like—may he excuse the expression—to ask pardon for the fruitful suffering he was exacting of me.

I also learned this lesson: I must be disposed to receive from the hands of Jesus, *everything,* everything that he may wish to send me; because all comes from his love and is ordered perfectly to do me good. Not only because I love him, but because I know that he loves me, I ought to receive tranquilly whatever he sends me.

At the same time I ought to receive everything with love, I ought to have an unalterable confidence in him in all the circumstances of my life. Nothing will be lacking to me; I shall have all that I need; strength to suffer, counsel to make decisions. It is enough for me to turn my eyes and my heart to Jesus to have what I need on all occasions. To be inclined toward all that Jesus sends and to trust him in everything and through everything, are these not the most solid bases of an unalterable peace?

Some days of aridity and others of consolation prepared for this grace, which kept increasing slowly, as if it were not possible to support it if it took place suddenly and all at once. Let us try to give some preliminary explanations.

Perhaps the most comprehensive definition of grace in general is this: grace is the seed of divine life. Grace is that divine life already, to be sure, but inchoate, incomplete, since it does not reach full development except in heaven. When we say that grace is the seed of the divine life, we understand the *integral* divine life, in the entire process of its development on earth until its consummation in heaven. In baptism we receive, in germ, all the graces of earth and all the glory of eternity. The whole secret of our sanctification lies in the development of that germ, in the cultivation of that seed.

What we affirm of grace in general, we can also apply to each grace in particular, especially to the graces that point out a new stage in the spiritual life and more especially to what we could call its *central grace.* All that precedes it is preparation; all that follows it is development and its effects.

For Archbishop Martínez, such was the grace of September 21, 1927; all the previous graces prepared for it and the twenty-eight years of his life afterwards were filled with the opulent fruits of that same grace. This is what can and should be called the *fourth stage*.

The division of the spiritual life into three stages is traditional: the purgative, illuminative and unitive ways. The unitive way culminates in the transforming union. But as we said already, the unitive way, the transforming union, the spiritual marriage, still are germs, but the most prolific, the most fecund, which should germinate and develop and produce the most exquisite fruits of sanctity.

It would be absurd, actually, if, when the soul reaches the highest union on earth, its life would stagnate, that it would remain permanently inactive. Just the contrary happens; that is the time when the action of the soul, under the motion of the Holy Spirit, reaches its maximum. This is the *fourth stage.*

It is true that the mystics are not accustomed to speak of it. A few years ago, when Father Poulain, S.J., was consulted about the matter, he answered: "Unfortunately, there is nothing written about the fourth stage.

But from the fact that there is nothing written about it one cannot conclude that it does not exist, and more so when the causes of this silence are understood. Among these causes the following may be pointed out:

1) It does not seem useful to speak of the fourth stage when so few souls actually reach these heights. It suffices that writers sketch the summit of the Christian life, like St. John of the Cross and St. Teresa, describing the main features of the spiritual marriage. Similarly, it would not be useful in an ordinary course in mathematics to treat of infinitesimal calculus; it would suffice to indicate that above ordinary mathematics there are still courses in higher mathematics.

2) It is not only useless, but it can be dangerous to speak of these heights to souls in general, for the imagination, especially the feminine, can conjure up dangerous illusions. Then they try to fly without wings, to "jump stages," believing themselves on

the heights, when they scarcely begin to take the first steps on solid ground. How much harm is done by false mysticism! What disparagement it casts upon true mysticism!

3) Even when it might be useful and could not be harmful to speak of the fourth stage, it is very difficult, if not impossible. How translate into coarse human language those sublime operations of grace? For that reason St. Thomas Aquinas no longer wished to continue writing at the end of his life; for that reason the mystics in their final days preferred to keep silent. St. Angela de Foligno has a revealing passage pertinent to this subject:

When God presents himself to the soul, when the Lord uncovers his face, the soul expands and he pours out into this suddenly enlarged capacity unheard-of joys and riches; and this takes place in an abyss of which I have not spoken until now. . . . Then the knowledge of God surpasses possibilities foreseen by the intelligence; and such is the light, and such is the evidence, and such is the new abyss, that it is inaccessible to the created heart. . . . It is impossible to say anything of this abyss; there is not a word whose sound gives any idea of it; there is not a thought nor an intellect that can venture up to it.[4]

But in what did that grace of September 21 consist? Let us recall what we indicated before. On September 21, 1916, the grace of spiritual betrothal was promised; on March 25, 1927, the transforming union (spiritual marriage) took place; and on September 21 of the same year, His Excellency received a grace of spiritual fecundity, like the complement and development of the transforming union.

All this can be explained in this way: in the transforming union, the soul is united with the Word. But this union is spiritually fecund; its fruit is Jesus, Jesus reproduced in the soul itself and, through its ministry, Jesus reproduced in the souls of others (apostolic life).

___

[4] *Le livre des visions et instructions de la B. Angèle de Foligno,* chap. 27.

To find the key which explains this mystery to us, we must have recourse to the mystery of the Incarnation, in which the divine Word was united to the sacred humanity. These are the nuptials celebrated by the heavenly Father; the nuptials of the Lamb of which the Apocalypse speaks (Apoc. 19:7); the nuptials that the king made for his son of whom the Gospel speaks (Matt. 22:2, 4, 9); those which the Canticle of Canticles celebrates with a divine nuptial song. Christian marriage, because it is a faint image of that union, is called by St. Paul "a great sacrament, but I speak in Christ and in the Church" (Eph. 5:32).

This union of the Word with the most sacred humanity was divinely fecund: its fruit was *Jesus*. Does not Jesus rise from the union of the divinity and the humanity in the Person of the Word?

The end of the Incarnation was the glory of the Father; but with this glory the salvation of man was intertwined and, consequently, his justification and his sanctification. Therefore the Incarnation, sin being presupposed, had the Redemption as a necessary complement. And so we affirm in the Creed that the Son of God, for our salvation, took flesh and became man.

Jesus Christ redeemed us by his sacrifice, whereby he merited for us the grace that purifies us from sin and incorporates us with him so that we may live his very life. Thus, incorporated with Christ, living his very life, vivified by his own Spirit, we form the whole Christ, the full Christ; we constitute the Mystical Body of which he is the Head; mystically we become Jesus. *"Christus facti sumus,"* as St. Augustine says.

As that union with Christ, our life, makes charity the final term, and as charity is the love of friendship and this demands the likeness of the friends, one understands that we cannot be united to Christ without having a likeness with him, at least an incipient likeness. But afterwards likeness and union grow parallel, the more united, the more similar; the more similar, the more united. The summit of union is also in the likeness; it is already a transformation. Therefore it is called transforming union.

The mystery of the Incarnation is, I repeat, the key which explains it. Just as the sun is a focus of light whose rays illumine the whole earth, so the mystery of the Incarnation is a union which is reflected in every soul in the state of grace. There the Word is united hypostatically with the sacred humanity; here the Word is united, by means of his humanity, with all the elect. Our humanity comes to be a prolongation of his.[5] And so the mystery of the Incarnation has a certain reflection in all souls, and in the measure that the union becomes more intimate and the likeness more finished, the reflection of the Incarnation is more perfect. It is Jesus who in a certain manner is born again, to reproduce his life, to live his mysteries, and to accomplish his work, which is always to glorify the Father and to save men. Such is the fecundity of the transforming union.

The fourth stage is nothing else than that very prolific period when the transformed soul produces its fruits. In the soul itself, the virtues of Christ are reproduced,[6] the mysteries of his life are renewed mystically, especially his sacrifice. The soul, in turn, obtains graces for others, so that Jesus may be formed in them, sinners converted and the just sanctified. It is necessary "to be Jesus to do the work of Jesus," according to the felicitous expression of Monsignor Gay, and it is also true that the soul, who through the transforming union is Jesus, cannot stop doing the work of Jesus. Thus, our Lord said to St. Catherine de Ricci: "Through you I continue saving the world."

Ordinarily, a soul reproduces a special mystery. For example,

[5] According to the beautiful expression of Sister Elizabeth of the Trinity, "a superadded humanity."

[6] They are not the ordinary virtues, but those exercised under the influence of the Holy Spirit, which St. Thomas calls *"iam purgati animi,"* i.e., proper to souls already purified.

St. Thérèse manifested the divine infancy. She acquired a simplicity, an ingenuity, a candor, a childlike confidence, in spite of maturity of years. Another reproduces his Passion, now with tremendous interior sufferings, now with terrible infirmities, now with sufferings caused by men. On some holy souls God has miraculously impressed the wounds of Christ; but many who have no exterior marks can say with St. Paul: "I bear in my body the wounds of our Lord Jesus Christ" (Gal. 6:17).

Some souls reproduce the Eucharistic mystery with their life of constant oblation, of perpetual immolation, of silence, of solitude, of annihilation. Others reproduce his apostolic life: it is Jesus who travels again the paths of this life, preaching goodness, preaching peace; and the sick recover health, and the dead through sin rise, and the deaf hear that irresistible word, and the blind open their eyes to the light of faith, and the paralytics, who lie in inaction, are converted into apostles, and the poor have the Gospel preached to them (Matt. 11:5).

Perhaps this brief explanation will give some remote idea of the fourth stage which His Excellency entered, so we think, on September 21, 1927. We find nothing written about this day, but each year he observed the anniversary with faithful gratitude and frequently, in his personal notes, he refers to this grace as the central and the greatest of his life. He did not write about it because it was, no doubt, something inexpressible. However, there are some lines written a few days before, which give us an inkling of what happened afterwards.

From First Vespers of today the rapturous grace that I have just received began.

Yesterday, during an arid prayer, I wanted to find something practical to profit by and so I tried to think about how I ought to love Jesus. Suddenly an intense, tender love came into my soul with special characteristics of disinterestedness and delicacy. I felt a sweet, overwhelming desire of giving pleasure to Jesus, of not bothering him, of not hurting him, of always being content with what he might give and of smiling graciously. To receive what he gives me and to give him what he asks of me; but with peace, with joy, always satisfied with him, pleased with his will, rejoicing in his felicity.

I cannot express what I felt. Not to want consolations when he does not give them so as not to bother him; to have the finest behavior toward him so as not to wound him. I would like to change myself into something very soft for Jesus' feet lest they be hurt; I would like to change myself into tenderness to enfold him, lest he miss the Father's bosom, so that he might continue distilling his divine fragrance.

And I saw and understood that such love, that shade of love, is proper to maternal love. I remembered how my mother loved me. That delicacy is maternal! Is it possible that it exists in my heart? It is the shade, proper to the love of Mary and of Joseph. Maternal and paternal amount to the same when one deals with spiritual things. O Jesus, my Jesus, whom I wish to carry in my soul with the delicacy with which a mother carries her little one. O Jesus, when and how did you touch my heart?

Today I have a *new heart,* a heart that burns and is wounded. You know, my Beloved, that I wanted to love you the whole day today, to love you with great delicacy. You know what I mean. To love you with delicacy, I need to be very pure; you are accustomed to live in purity, to breathe purity. Bathe me with purity, impregnate me with purity so that I may love you as I want and as you wish, in a delicate, exquisite way.

I bear a sweet wound in my heart, O my adorable Jesus. I cannot express what you did to me today. How did you wound me? Was it a look of your eyes or a caress of your adorable hand?

I want to love you with adoration; I desire to adore you. Blessed be you who can be and who should be loved even to adoration!

But, let the pen cease from trying to express what the heart can scarcely feel.... Jesus, I love you, you know how...!

The new life of apostolic fruitfulness that Archbishop Martínez entered upon with the grace of September 21, 1927, is well described in a page taken from his spiritual exercises, made some time afterwards.

Yesterday turned out too practical. I got myself into a labyrinth of details by forming minutely precise resolutions. Today, very early, our Lord made me see that *that* is not the key to my spiritual life. How many times I have drawn up that kind of regulation of my life, uselessly! At least with little fruit.

God must give me the consummation in love. To please him, surely I will do what I can and what he may wish; but I ought to wait for everything from him and my firmest resolutions must tend rather *to letting myself be guided by him.*

Meticulous methods and practices are not profitable for *me* nor do I feel at home in them; what is useful for me is something simpler, higher, deeper.[7]

Without mincing words, ascetical practices are not the means to reach the consummation that both Jesus and I desire, but something—I will speak clearly—of a mystical character.[8] If he must do it, it falls to my lot:

a) to eliminate the ego and to lose my initiative; removing the obstacles pointed out (in the notes of the preceding day) will be a help.

b) to give myself up to God generously and to become docile and compliant to his inspirations.

c) to abase myself, to lose myself in God.

Later, reading the Commentary on the Epistle to the Ephesians,[9] I found what I was looking for: the three graces that St. Paul begged from the heavenly Father for the faithful (Eph. 3:16-19):

1) To be strengthened with power through his Spirit unto the

[7] His Excellency does not deny that these detailed methods and practices can do good to other souls, but he is convinced that he does not profit from them.

[8] After so many years he resolves to call the graces that he receives and needs *mystical*. Taking into account all circumstances, this confession is very important.

[9] Especially Dom Delatte, *Les Epîtres de St. Paul replacées dans le milieu historique des Actes des Apôtres.*

progress of the interior man. That is, to eliminate all the egoism of the old man so that the new one may appear, strong, spirited.

2) "To have Christ dwelling through faith in your hearts: rooted and grounded in love." This means that love, in all its fullness, attaches our soul to Christ in such a way that with our fickleness removed, we may allow ourselves, submissive and docile, to be ruled by him.

3) "That you may be able to comprehend with all the saints what is the breadth and length and height and depth, and to know Christ's love which surpasses all knowledge, in order that you may be filled unto all the fullness of God." That is, with egoism eliminated and intimately united to Christ by charity we may comprehend the mystery of Christ in its unspeakable dimensions, and thus arrive at that consummation in which God is all to the soul.

In summary: *fortitude* to destroy the old man; *charity* to work only under the influence of Jesus; heavenly *light* to penetrate the mystery of Christ. Hence, three petitions and resolutions:

1) To eliminate all that comes from the old man. Remove the three said obstacles for this purpose.

2) To give myself up lovingly to Jesus so that he may be my Master, ruling in such a way, that there may not be in me, as far as possible, movements other than those which he impresses and which I shall follow readily.

3) To study Jesus constantly and docilely that he may be the science of my soul and of my life.

I ought to wonder at the loving providence of God which impelled me, in spite of my vacillations, to take as reading for these days the Epistle to the Ephesians and made me read the said passage precisely on the day and at the moment that I needed it.[10]

During the final prayer of this day, as I felt fatigued, I asked Jesus to let me rest in him and with tender condescension he communicated to me a sweet, intimate prayer of rest.

[10] The Archbishop always relished in a special way this passage from St. Paul. He said that it contained the entire doctrine of the transforming union. He was gratified to see that the Epistle in the new Mass of the Sacred Heart contained this passage.

I saw how for my priestly life I need nothing else than the resolutions already made. I was thinking that yesterday would be a digression and that afterwards I should consider it relative to the priesthood; but if for my own individual life I ought to abase myself through love and surrender myself to the dispensations of my Master, with greater reason should I do this in relation to my ministry, because it is something personal to Jesus, the Supreme Priest, something to which I, by my own self, have no right.

We are ministers of Christ and dispensers of the mysteries of God. For the ministry, then, the old man should totally disappear and, if one may so speak, even the rational man. Jesus must work in me; I should be like an instrument that operates when driven, which has neither initiative nor personality and whose merit consists in being docile and pliable so as to keep the action of the one who moves it in its integrity and purity.

Neither for liturgical functions, nor for the direction of souls, nor for the government of the diocese, should I do anything but disappear totally, allowing Jesus to work freely in me, and enter fully into the mystery of Christ.

In all the preceding notes we see the characteristics of the mystical life. When the gifts predominate in a soul, the Holy Spirit moves the soul directly. Hence, the essentially *passive* character of the mystical life. But that passivity, far from being inaction, is just the contrary; never is the activity of the soul so great, so efficacious, so fruitful, as when it is moved by the Holy Spirit. Then it does not walk step by step; it flies.

This evening, the Vigil of Pentecost, without my trying or foreseeing it, the Holy Spirit took charge of me. Scarcely did I surrender, as customarily, to his love and his action, than I felt a pure, holy invasion, and he gave me to understand *experimentally* that divine life which has been the theme of my exercises.

His breath of love drew me and carried me from the Son to the Father, uniting me closely with Jesus and making me rest in the bosom of the Father.

This life is a true heaven, because it is a participation in the life of God. From those heights, I saw everything in a new way, full of God; and in the light of the Spirit, everything earthly was transformed into something divine and everything prosaic was idealized in a celestial manner.

In the final period of prayer I surrendered myself fully to love—how many times I probably surrendered myself to egoism, to vanity!—and I felt happy in having the Holy Spirit as Master, and I gave myself up to his action with all the docility of my soul. May he possess me and rule me; may he introduce me into the bosom of God and take me as the instrument of his action and immolate me, if it please him.

A few days later, in his private notes, he rectifies this rather strong expression: "How many times I probably surrendered myself to egoism, to vanity." "Thanks be to God," he says, "it is not true, for although many times I made room for those things, I never gave myself up to them. I said one thing for another."

I arose at daybreak with the conviction that the Holy Spirit had come to my soul; I feel a new docility.

I saw the Holy Spirit as the spouse of my soul. He fecundates it in an ineffable manner, forming Jesus therein. My soul needs all affections, all tones of love. None of them alone suffices for it, because it was made for all.

In divine love all shades of human affections are unified. I felt the pure, holy, nuptial love; I felt happiness that the Holy Spirit unites himself to me and communicates fecundity to my soul so as to form, or to finish forming, Jesus in me.

I now understand the liturgical prayer, "May the effusion of the Holy Spirit, O Lord, purify our hearts and fertilize them with the interior sprinkling of thy divine dew."

Love, fidelity, union are the duties of the soul.

The idea hinted at before has been clarified and made more precise: the soul needs all shades of love, because it was made for all, because it bears within, secret desires for them all. The supernatural life must not be inferior to the natural life in this point; especially the life of a soul totally consecrated to God should not, cannot be the least envious of the one who embraced a less perfect life. Not a single one of the shades of love must be lacking to the soul for whom God is all. By consecrating oneself to him, one loses nothing and gains much; one gains when he goes from the sketch to the reality.

No desire of the heart must remain unfulfilled in heaven; otherwise there would not be complete happiness. The life of grace is substantially that of glory. . . . Therefore, divine love must embrace all shades of love, perfected and unified.

There is one shade that our heart necessarily longs for, it is the reflection of the paternity of the Father. Virgin souls do not have to relinquish it. In their interior life this shade is holier and more perfect, because their fecundity is richer and more excellent: it has Jesus as its end. This is not a simple metaphor, but a mystery, a reality. The whole Christ is not only the one born of Mary, but the one born unceasingly in the Church, the one formed in all the elect.

St. Paul explains this doctrine many times. In the Epistle to the Ephesians, he says: "For building up the body of Christ, until we all attain to the unity of faith and of the deep knowledge of the Son of God, to perfect manhood, to the mature measure of the fullness of Christ" (Eph. 4:13).

In another place the same Apostle says: "My dear children, with whom I am in labor again, until Christ is formed in you" (Gal. 4:19). This admirable paternity relates to others and to ourselves and has as its end Christ who is formed in us. "We are changed into Christ," according to the expression of St. Augustine. It has also been said: "The Christian is another Christ." And this—I must repeat it—is not a simple metaphor; it is a mysterious reality.

No doubt the Holy Spirit forms in us, but we cooperate in his formation in a similar, though very remote manner, to the way Mary cooperated in the formation of Jesus in his real body.

Jesus is, consequently, *our son mystically,* and the secret longing of our heart is satisfied with this tender, disinterested love, full of abnegation and of delicacy, the reflection of the Father's love.

Everything is elevated and ennobled when we understand this love: our work of sanctification stops being the work of perfecting ourselves; it is the work of forming Jesus in us, caring for him, of making him grow, of bringing him up to the fullness of his age and of his stature. Legitimate and holy self-love is turned into purest maternal love. I love myself, because I love Jesus; I care for myself, because I care for Jesus; I sanctify myself so that in me Jesus may attain his plenitude.

If, after considering Jesus in myself, I consider him in others, the apostolic life takes on the exalted proportions of a paternity such as St. Paul conceived it. Considered in this way, how can flesh and blood and human designs be seen in the holy affection for souls, in the exquisite work of forming Christ in them?

The apostolic life is converted into a life of tenderness and holy docility to the Holy Spirit, the only one who can form Jesus. When exercising this participation in the divine paternity, it is necessary to penetrate deeply into the mystery of Christ.

My three resolutions are exalted and take on a more divine meaning, if one may so speak.

My exercises terminated with the elevation of my soul to the heavenly Father in whom everything is consummated, because he is the beginning of all things. For him love takes a sweet tone of filial affection which the Holy Spirit breathes into us, making us cry Abba! Father!

This filial affection is most appropriate for the creature, the best adapted to our heart; it is our basic affection. It is the affection of *nothingness* before the *plenitude* which, by an excess of mercy, our adoption as sons in Jesus Christ gave to us.

A son is a being who received the life of love from a father. That concept is never accomplished so perfectly as in our filiation with respect to God, from whom we receive everything as the fruit of an incomparable love. I analyzed that love of the Father and I could see what ought to be our love for him.

It is a *gratuitous* love, infinitely gratuitous. "He chose us before the foundation of the world" (Eph. 1:4), when we were nothing, when we had neither merit nor attraction, nor title to love. And precisely on that account, this love becomes extraordinary before our eyes; only an infinite love, a love *per se*[11] can be fixed on nothingness. "Therefore I love my nothingness," says Dom Delatte, "because I love God." Our filial love should be as deep as our nothingness, as deep as that infinitely gratuitous love.

Because the Father loved us who were nothingness, his love has complete certainty, divine constancy. If he loved us when we were nothingness, he will continue loving, although we have neither attractiveness nor a title to being love.

When someone knows he is loved because of some natural endowment, he cares for it painstakingly; and if the gift is a frail thing, he lives in constant fear of losing the love, by losing the title to it. I once read that a beautiful woman was on the point of blinding the one she loved so that he might never see the decadence of her youth. As our title to the Father's love is our nothingness, we are sure of that love, because nothing can tear that title away from us. We can glory in our misery because it is the enticement of divine love.

Since that love is secure, our love for the Father is impregnated with *confidence*. Such is filial love. Confidence fails either because we fear not being loved, or because we doubt lest something in us diminish the love which has been given to us. These motives for distrust do not fit between nothingness and plenitude. The smaller the loved one and the greater the lover, the more trustful is love.

The Father's love is most *tender*. I think tenderness presupposes weakness. When one loves a small, weak being, tenderness springs up; and perhaps this being, also loves greatness and majesty in the same way.

Finally, the love of the Father is characterized by an unspeakable impression of *repose,* because nothingness is cast into plenitude, for beings rest when they return to their beginning; and the Father is the beginning in heaven and on earth.

With what vehemence I felt the necessity of the action of grace when I placed my soul in contact with the beginning from whom proceeds every gift, every grace, all love. The action of grace is

[11] That which has in itself its origin and reason for being.

linked by divine logic, with adoration, with supplication, with all the essential duties of the creature toward its God.

All shades of love were blended in my heart in that supreme act of my soul, which was the inexpressible *Amen* of those days and which was buried in the bosom of the one, triune God, to whom be glory and honor world without end. Amen, Amen!

When a soul has reached these heights, it is confirmed in humility, as it were, so that it cannot be vain of the graces received. It is impossible for those shadows that imply the lack of humility to exist in the midst of such great light. It is related of St. Angela de Foligno that on one occasion God spoke to her such words of love that she, thinking about her sins and defects, believed herself unworthy of such great love and, beginning to doubt, she said to the one speaking to her: "If you were the Holy Spirit, you would not say such things to me, because I am frail and capable of pride."

And the Lord answered her: "Let's see, try to be vain on account of my words; come on, try to do it, try a little!"

"I made every effort to conceive a sentiment of pride," the Saint confesses, "but my sins came to my memory and I felt a humility such as I have never felt in my life."[12]

On the other hand, a delicate sentiment usually called "spiritual modesty" is very proper to this stage. When the soul contemplates the graces with which God has enriched it, especially when he makes it experience how much he loves it, when his love takes complacency in it, and rests therein, the soul feels an immense, tender shame, and should like to hide, to bury itself to annihilate itself. We find this sentiment in the soul of Archbishop Martínez.

I keep on adjusting myself to that difficult humility of which I have spoken in another place. During the past days, after feeling the weight of my famous misery, I went to the chapel during the

[12] *Op. cit.*

night and scarcely did I kneel down that our Lord made me feel the purity of my soul in so deep and clear a way, that I conceived a *new confidence,* tender and sweet as that of a child, which made me throw myself into the heart of Jesus with unbounded confidence.

The other day, I had fulfilled my resolution and I had kept calm and content that at any rate Jesus loves me and—who would believe it?—he made me feel that he not only loved me the same, but that my soul was pleasing to him.

What a delightful embarrassment I felt! I had to "turn the page" because I could take no more. This was in the train, returning from Mexico City to Morelia.

Apropos of the sermon for the feast of St. Rose of Lima,[13] Canon Buitrón, my old friend, said to me, contrary to his custom, that my facility in preaching and writing was extraordinary, because he had witnessed many things, among them, that on one occasion I wrote a sermon while I smoked a cigar.

I had not paid any attention to that, I said to him; I had indeed noticed that facility, but I did not think it extraordinary.

And he answered me: "Yes, in many things you have not realized what God has given you and the special roads through which he is taking you. If you do not arrive at sanctity, you deserve to be beaten."

How those words helped me! I have meditated upon them and they have even made me fearful, but especially, greatly embarrassed!

It is certain that Canon Buitrón did not know the interior life of Archbishop Martínez, for while he lived, it was a rigidly guarded secret.

A new shame! I then caught on to the *why* of all my miseries. Perhaps without them I might become vain of all that God has wrought in me. The Lord guards his gifts with a fence of thorns.

A soul of election was undergoing terrible interior suffering, and I said to God—what shame it gives me even to write it!—

[13] Sermon in the Cathedral of Mexico City, August 30, 1935, arranged by the Embassy of Peru for the entire diplomatic Corps.

that through the love he had for me, would he give rest to that soul? And, as I found out later, its pains were turned into sweet consolations at that moment. No one can imagine the impression this produced upon me. Notwithstanding, the soul to whom I refer had to keep on thinking that I paid no attention, for I am a master in dissimulating my thoughts. First, I felt an immense gratitude with an embarrassment of the same magnitude. Afterwards an ardent love, the kind that fills the soul.

But more than the proof of love that Jesus gave me, the thought has reached my soul, especially lately, that my love satisfies him. Now I want to love him more and in a more refined, exquisite way, only for him.

I have felt very united to Jesus. Precisely last night and this morning, I saw most clearly that my miseries, anxieties and sufferings are something superficial; in the depth of my soul there is union, and consequently, a profound peace.

I feel a deep attraction for purity in its highest degree. I do not dare to acknowledge the purity of my soul—so much earthly dust has fallen into it!—but I cannot deny that God often seems to have revealed to me what is strange, what I do not comprehend . . . that my soul is pure, participating in Jesus' incomparable purity.

For a long time I have not felt spiritual joy at night. I cannot say what I felt, my eyes fastened on the ciborium; my heart fixed on the Holy Eucharist. Jesus united himself with me, God was mine, but adapted to my smallness through the most holy humanity of Jesus. They were moments of heaven.

Some days later, during private exposition of the Blessed Sacrament in my oratory, I received a most vivid light, and I discovered myself, which is as great as "discovering the Mediterranean."[14] I saw that there are two parts in me: one exterior, full of imperfections, which is the wrapping of another interior part, formed by God, which encloses the fruit of his graces, especially my grace of March 25 and of September 21, 1927. That part is pure, beautiful, and I did not know it.

[14] Famous expression of Chesterton.

In reality I did not believe deeply or at least I did not give importance to the aforementioned grace and to certain manifestations of God in respect to the purity of my soul, because I saw all that incompatible with my miseries.

But when with God's light I discerned both parts, my eyes were opened and I saw the truth. I believed interiorly (in the graces of God), without losing my fondness for my rags. Now, indeed, I am satisfied: I look inside, and I see the work of God, and I rejoice on account of it; I see the wrapping, and I take satisfaction in my miseries, without the one thing disturbing the other.

Now, indeed, I am going to devote myself to *living* my grace (the one of March 25 and of September 21) and develop it in my soul, without giving up my satisfaction in my tatters.

What it is to possess the truth! What it is to have one's eyes opened! What God's light can do! No wonder I could not harmonize things that were clear to me, yet seemingly incompatible; I had not discovered myself![15]

[15] We may know a truth by reason, but when God gives us to know it by a light of the mystical order, it seems to us as new as if we had never known it. Notice that His Excellency began to give this grace of 1927 its true importance, eight years afterwards! "There is a slowness in souls that we must respect," says Dom Delatte. God is the first in doing so; he accommodates himself to our weakness.

CHAPTER VI

Apostolate

THERE IS abundant evidence of the spiritual fruitfulness of the life of Archbishop Martínez. His field of action gradually became broader. After he had been Auxiliary Bishop of the Archdiocese of Morelia for fourteen years, he was named Co-adjutor to the Archbishop of Morelia on March 10, 1934.

On May 19, 1936, Most Reverend Pascual Díaz, Archbishop of Mexico, died. Archbishop Martínez was in the city on those days attending the obsequies and the burial. Everyone began to point to him as the most likely prelate to occupy the vacant See. And so it happened in fact. He was named Archbishop of Mexico on February 20, 1937. He took possession on April 14, the Solemnity of St. Joseph, and on February 14, 1938, Archbishop Leopoldo Ruiz vested him with the pallium in the Basilica of Tepeyac.

On August 9, 1937, the Holy Father placed him in charge of the affairs of the Apostolic Delegation; that is to say, at the same time that he was governing the foremost archdiocese in Mexico—with more than four million Catholics—he also was representing the Holy See in that country. Archbishop Martínez discharged this latter duty until 1949, when he asked the Holy See to send an Apostolic Delegate, for with the current peaceful relations between the civil and the ecclesiastical authorities, there were no complications to fear.

In 1950, at the death of Monsignor José Ignacio Márquez, the Holy See appointed Archbishop Martínez Pontifical Director of Mexican Catholic Action. On October 20, 1945, he was named Assistant at the Papal Throne and on June 29, 1951, he was appointed Archbishop Primate.

Since Archbishop Leopoldo Ruiz, while Archbishop of Morelia, was in exile for the greater part of the period, Archbishop Martínez actually governed the Archdiocese of Morelia; for this work Archbishop Ruiz gave him all the powers and the broadest liberty. In order to form some idea of his activity during that epoch, let us take at random the paragraph in which he writes a chronicle of those days for an intimate friend.

In June I left for Cortazar, a village near Celaya, to preach on the feast of the Sacred Heart; on the twenty-fourth I began my spiritual exercises, to finish them with Mass on the second of July. On the third of July I went to preach at Acámbaro for the next day's feast; immediately I left for Puruagüita, a parish near Acámbaro, to preach on the octave of St. Peter. On the seventh I left for Pénjamo to give some triple exercises from the ninth to the fifteenth; during the morning I gave two talks to the young ladies, two in the afternoon to the women, and two at night to the men. I heard as many confessions as I could and administered confirmation. On the sixteenth I preached for the feast of Our Lady of Mount Carmel—it was also a high Mass; on the seventeenth I returned to Morelia to receive two bishops and on the twenty-first I went back to Acámbaro to attend a gathering of priests associated with Catholic Action. From there I went to Tarandacuao to preach on the feast of St. James and I returned to Morelia on the twenty-sixth to dispose myself for peace some few days.[1]

During the first days of August I gave a retreat to the members of the Alliance of Love; afterwards I went to Celaya to a Catholic Action convention; from there to León to give the retreat to the Religious of the Cross. The very day that I returned to Morelia I began the retreat for the ladies of the "Home Crusade" and for the twenty-fourth I shall go to Celaya to preach in the Church of the Merced.[2]

[1] Letter of July, 1936.
[2] Letter of September 20, 1936.

His Excellency accomplished all this without neglecting the rectorship of the seminary, the government of the archdiocese and the pastoral visits throughout his vast territory.

During Lent his work was intensified. Throughout most of his priestly life he was accustomed to give series of retreats from Ash Wednesday until Palm Sunday, and occasionally more than one at a time, apart from the sermons of Holy Week. Crowds attended these services, sometimes as many as two and three thousand persons.

When His Excellency came to the Archdiocese of Mexico, it was natural that his work was doubled, even tripled, for his zeal embraced not only his entire archdiocese but all of Mexico. He accepted unhesitatingly all invitations to preach, wherever it might be, within or without the country, unless he had some previous engagement.

Who can count the number of confirmations in the thirty-two years and more of his episcopate? In one simple pastoral visit he affirmed that he had confirmed more than seven thousand persons; the weekly average of confirmations in the capital was from two to three thousand. Three days before his final illness he still went to the cathedral to confer confirmation.

Some thought it strange that His Excellency never relinquished this heavy task, since he had two auxiliary bishops and also the privilege of delegating the power of administering confirmation to other high-ranking ecclesiastics. During his life no one discovered the secret; but it was very simple. At the time of his consecration he formed the resolution to allot all the stipends that he might receive for administering the sacrament of confirmation to help the poor, especially the beggars.[3] Therefore, he never gave up that ministry; and already ill, he dragged himself to discharge it even to the end; his poor needed that alms. Is this not truly heroic? One knows not which to

[3] This resolution was written in his personal notes as well as the statement that he had kept it.

admire the more, his charity carried to the utmost limit or the inviolable silence with which he guarded his secret, although it did not escape him that some might judge his conduct unfavorably.

His day was completely filled from the time he arose until after midnight. He almost never retired before one o'clock in the morning. On one occasion he asked for an attendant at the Scholasticate of the Holy Spirit. The young religious assigned to accompany him in all his ministries that day, went from surprise to surprise, for the audiences, ministrations, sermons and other occupations succeeded one another without interruption. At ten o'clock at night, overcome by fatigue, he took leave of the Archbishop, but he could not refrain from asking him: "Your Excellency, do you have many days as busy as this one?"

"No; I have no more than 365 days a year like this one and 366 in leap year."

Many have asked how it was possible for the Archbishop, in the midst of so much activity, to write books. His apostolate of the pen was one of his most important works; it will immortalize his apostolic action. It was upon the advice of Bishop Banegas that Father Martínez began writing out his sermons, at least those of some importance. He had such a retentive memory that he learned them by heart, simply by writing them out.

When *La Cruz,* a review devoted exclusively to the spiritual life, appeared in January, 1921, Father Martínez collaborated with it and some article of his appeared in each monthly issue. During the two epochs of persecution, from 1914 to 1918 and from 1926 to 1929, he was obliged to keep hidden; thus, he had free time for writing. Afterward, involved in the avalanche of ministerial duties, it was almost impossible for him to write, except on rare occasions. When asked how he could write books in the midst of such great occupations, he answered, "I do not write books, I speak them!"

The writings of the Archbishop may be classified in three groups: (1) those that he wrote with his own hand; (2) those that he wrote in the same way, but were addressed to a particular person or to a religious, and consequently had to be adapted for publication; (3) those that he spoke in retreats, conversations, Spiritual Exercises, sermons and the like. These were taken down stenographically and afterwards edited, not in regard to matter, but in regard to form, since the spoken style is not the same as the written. These facts explain the inequality of style which any observer can detect in his writings. To clarify this point, let us discuss some of his works.

Archbishop Martínez' first printed book was *El Espíritu Santo,* published by *La Cruz* in 1939. It has already reached four editions in Spanish.[4] The sections, "True Devotion to the Holy Spirit" and "The Beatitudes" belong to the first group of writings; those on the gifts and the fruits of the Holy Spirit belong to the third. This work is a complete treatise on the Holy Spirit. Without fear of exaggeration, we can affirm that it is the best that has been written to expound the theology of the Holy Spirit, so little known among the faithful. Although based on tradition, especially on St. Thomas Aquinas, the work has great originality. It is evident that it could not have been written except with the supernatural lights of contemplation.

When Archbishop Martínez realized the good that his first book was doing for souls, he gave freedom to the editor of *La Cruz* to publish his works according to the latter's selection, with title and arrangement of his choice. Thus, there appeared the volume, *Jesús,* which has now reached six Spanish editions.[5] The first part, "Teachings of Jesus" belongs to the first classification of his writings, with the exception of the "Paths of Peace," "Silence of Jesus," and "How to Console Jesus," which belong to the third group; the remainder of the book belongs

[4] English edition: *The Sanctifier.* St. Anthony Guild Press, 1958. (*Trans.*)
[5] English edition: *Only Jesus,* B. Herder Book Co., 1962 (*Trans.*)

to the second group of writings. *La Cruz* announced this work with these comments: "It will be Archbishop Martínez' masterpiece. For solid doctrine, penetrating unction, profound genuine mysticism, and elevated style, it contains pages comparable to those of Monsignor Gay, Père Lacordaire and Dom Marmion."

The Archbishop wrote his approbation of this book: "In reference to my last book, *Jesús, La Cruz* states that it is my masterpiece. This enthralls me, not on account of the praise but, Jesus being my soul's Beloved, my great satisfaction will be that what I have written about him is my masterpiece, the work dear to my heart."

And in another place he states: "Now the first edition of *Jesús* is out. Surely this book is going to be my favorite by its very title. It treats of *him!* Although in reality one is always treating of him, there is a very sweet attraction in dealing directly of him!"

Closely following *Jesús,* was the publication of *La Pureza en el Ciclo Litúrgico*,[6] an original study treating of the relationship of purity with each of the stages of the liturgical cycle. The chapters belong predominantly to the first group of writings.

Next in appearance was *Simientas Divinas*, a title changed in the four succeeding editions to *Vida Espiritual*.[7] It contains a remarkable treatise on "Desolations," which has been of great benefit to souls.

Additional works of Archbishop Martínez not yet translated into English are: *A Propósito De Un Viaje, Santa María de Guadalupe, El Sacerdote, Misterio De Amor, Almas Proceres, La Intimidad Con Jesús, El Camino Regio Del Amor, and Ven Jesús.*

The principal characteristic to be noted in Archbishop Martínez' writings is this: they do not have a scientific, literary, erudite purpose; they are essentially apostolic. Through these

[6] English edition: *Liturgical Preludes,* The Peter Reilly Co., 1961 (*Trans.*)
[7] English edition: *Secrets of the Interior Life,* B. Herder, 1949 (*Trans.*)

works he exemplified St. Thomas' definition of the apostolic
life. "To contemplate and to give to others the fruits of contemplation." Archbishop Martínez did just that. Therefore, his
writings have a captivating unction, a contagious fervor, and a
vibrant love for souls.

They alone would suffice, not only to immortalize his name
—a matter about which he was not concerned—but to immortalize his apostolic life, forever doing good to souls. How many
persons will find that these pages open up new horizons, expand the soul, increase trust and inflame love. Death has not
sealed his lips. He will continue speaking through his works of
his divine obsession, of his holy folly, of *love!*

Archbishop Martínez was also an apostle of the spoken word.
If he had been told that he was an orator of the style of Lacordaire by his eloquence or of Bossuet by his elevated thought,
he would have protested. No, he preached as an apostle "not in
the persuasive words of human wisdom but in the demonstration of the Spirit" (I Cor. 1:4).

"I heard a sermon," he writes in his personal notes, "an eloquent, impressive address; but it was a human discourse, not
supernatural, not priestly. Then I realized how one ought to
preach, not with the persuasive words of human eloquence but
with the demonstration of the Spirit. Not only preaching, but
all ministerial works should be so: totally supernatural. The
same applies even to the ordinary acts of the priest. Everything
in us ought to be supernatural, sacerdotal; in all things we
should be other Christs."

His Excellency prepared his sermons during prayer, that is,
during prayer he received the lights that afterwards he eluci-
dated in his sermons. Here are some proofs:

On the third of the month, at night, I began thinking about the
sermon for the next day, feast of Our Lady Refuge of Sinners, and
when my mind reached a point that referred directly to Jesus—
that however pure, beautiful and loving the Holy Virgin may be,

we would neither love her as we do, nor would she attract us so irresistibly, if she were not the Mother, the Depositary, the Distributor of Jesus, since he fills everything,—when my mind reached this idea, I repeat, I was so moved that I could not go on.

On the fifteenth of August, Mary most holy gave me two gifts. When I began to read the lessons for the first nocturn of the feast, from the Canticle of Canticles, I understood in a new, synthetic way this book of Scripture. I saw how it expresses all the tones of love, its joys and delights; how divine love realizes them in a form superior to human love, in a spiritual, lofty, heavenly way. He who loves need not envy those who enjoy human affections; divine love accomplishes all the charms of the latter in an eminent, superior way.

The Canticle of Canticles, read superficially, is an idyll of human love; interpreted deeply, it is an idyll of divine love. It reproduces all the attractions of human love, surpassing them immensely and adding to them new charms reserved to divine love. This, no doubt is very well known; but when God illuminates what we already know, he imparts to it an ineffable novelty. How many new things we discover in the old, in God's light!

The other gift of the Virgin was an inspiration for a sermon. In one point I saw all that I had to say; it was something new and rich in meaning. In regard to a sermon for the high Mass, I saw how the expression of St. Paul applied to the priest: "I live now, not I, but Christ." He lives in us whenever we are exercising any act of the ministry. He must live in us always, even in our ordinary actions. At each moment we ought to live sacerdotally.

Now I have, indeed, suffered a little. I believe that there are sacerdotal sufferings, sufferings for souls. I have one affair, especially, in which the devil probably has a part.

Owing to those little pains, perhaps, God gave me light to form a deeper concept of the happiness of this life, which I may express in these words: the happiness of this life consists in sacrificing self for others. I knew this, of course, and even had preached it; but when God teaches, the entire doctrine is new.

I notice the different concepts of happiness that we customarily form for ourselves throughout life; they constitute a graduation. First, we think that happiness consists in the discreet, well-ordered use of the goods which God gives us, in the "golden mean" of the Latin poet, but Chistianized.

Afterwards, happiness presents itself as based in detachment from all created things, thus giving us a blessed liberty and making us capable of establishing ourselves in the true Good.

Later on, we understand that love is happiness; but we conceive of love rather as our own good than as the good of the Beloved. Finally, the concept of love is purified and we come to understand that the most exquisite thing about love, in this world, is sacrifice. And so we build up the lofty, profound concept that to be happy is to sacrifice oneself for love.

The Archbishop preached these truths many times; he had become acquainted with them through supernatural light. Later on, our Lord completed this teaching.

A few days afterward, some persons behaved toward me with impertinence; not a major offense, but one of those trifles that hurt. Our Lord gave me light in prayer to ask with singular charity and great earnestness for graces for those persons; but not simply as fulfilling a duty, but satisfying the heart's need.

I then glimpsed something of the divine heart of Jesus, for I do not doubt that what I felt was a participation of his interior sentiments. He must feel like that, for his love is embittered, so to speak, with ingratitude, yet he is moved to bestow graces liberally upon those who wound him.

Is not this heroic charity? In another place he says:

We behave toward Jesus with great trust. I tell him many things that I was unconsciously hiding from him before; I have even varied my expression a little. In fact, for some time, when I am going to preach, to write, or transact some business, I address the Holy Spirit, surrendering myself to his love and to his action; I ask the Word to unite himself to me and speak through my mouth and

I hasten to the Father, offering Jesus for the souls whom I am about to address.

Now, I am asking a caress of light, of purity and of love for souls. Love keeps dominating in my life. I tell our Lord that I want to do nothing else but love him. I desire that love to take three forms in me, conformably to the Beloved's good pleasure: that he unite me to himself, that he use me for the good of souls, and that he immolate me according to his will.

The other day, because of something that I read, an immense gratitude overcame me, because he loved me with predilection and he chose me for his love and for his work. How much he has to do to make me his! Beyond a doubt, I needed Jesus; only he could love and endure me; for my misery needed his mercy; the aspirations of my heart needed his beauty, kindness and love.

In this state I try to speak with him whenever I can, to praise his beauty and to preach his love. What one feels in the pulpit when the soul is filled with love! On Good Friday I preached, taking as a text, the first verse of the Canticle of Canticles. I was very satisfied because I poured out my heart in praising him and I believe that he, also, was content in spite of my deficiencies.

On Easter Sunday I also spoke with him of the joy of the Resurrection; certainly I went to preach almost without knowing what to say; but he helps me and at times speaks through my mouth.

On another occasion he makes this ingenuous confession: "God has granted me on these days a kind of profound feeling of faith, the work of the gift of understanding, no doubt. In the retreats I have preached on the theological virtues with special pleasure."

In fact, he insisted strongly in his sermons upon the theological virtues. He realized that, through the tendency of being too practical, preachers spoke very little of those virtues, whose importance is capital, nevertheless. He used to say that although it might seem paradoxical, the most speculative principles are in reality the most practical, because they have wider application in practice. This is seen very clearly in moral theology, for example; the fundamental principles are the most necessary for the resolution of practical cases. Such are the theological virtues; if they do not intervene at each step in our daily, practical life, the latter loses its supernatural character. In this, Archbishop Martínez was, at least in Mexico, an innovator in a certain sense.

His heart was so full of divine love, it was impossible not to betray his strictly guarded secret, at least in part, when he was preaching. Let us see some examples.

Several times when I have spoken in public the love I have for Jesus was exposed to view. Although this disclosure of my secret pains me, on the other hand it is gratifying to be convinced that I love him. It is delightful to discover, to touch the reality of our love. If others perceive the perfume of roses, the real roses are those that we carry.

One day (it pains me even to write it) I gave a conference in a private home. Each week some intellectual gives a secular address on art, science, or the like. One day they invited me. In the talk I told them that I was not a lecturer but a preacher; that like St. Paul, I wanted to know nothing more than Jesus. So I spoke to them of some features of his spiritual physiognomy, of how seemingly incompatible qualities were harmoniously joined in him: humility and magnanimity, simplicity and prudence, energy and gentleness.

The conference was well received and some persons told me that I had painted my own portrait in delineating Jesus. A courtesy, no doubt; but how much their remark pleased me—although it might be through courtesy—that I resemble Jesus! He who loves understands what I am saying.

Two seasons of the ecclesiastical year, Christmas and Holy Week, showered Archbishop Martínez with such lights and effusions of divine love that he could not withstand more. One Holy Week his heart was so inundated with love that he needed an outlet, so he went to preach the customary Holy Hour on

Holy Thursday evening for the Religious of the Cross. When he finished, he realized that he had spoken one hour and forty minutes. Neither he nor they had noticed it; he was not exhausted nor were the religious tired.

Another form of the Archbishop's apostolate was spiritual direction, especially of souls of election. Here, perhaps, is the field in which the fruitfulness of his apostolate reached its maximum. For if one act of love of God gives him more glory than all external works, as St. John of the Cross teaches, we may also conclude that more glory is given to him and more benefit redounds to the Church by carrying a soul to the heights of God's love than by converting many sinners.

The words of the Gospel, "There will be more joy in heaven upon one sinner doing penance than upon ninety-nine just who need not penance," do not oppose this statement. For, either these words have a fine irony, calling the Pharisees just, or they treat of the just in general, the entire flock. It is evident that there is no need of a welcome party for the sheep that have not strayed away, but only for the lost one that has returned to the fold. Beyond a doubt, a truly holy soul gives more glory to God than the simple conversion of ninety-nine sinners. It suffices to cite the Blessed Virgin, for whose immaculate conception and sanctity heaven has rejoiced more than for all converted sinners.

Archbishop Martínez had such a degree of spiritual fecundity that he bore not one, but several souls to the heights of perfection, insofar as it is humanly possible to judge. He himself, in his notes, frequently recognizes as one of the greatest predilections God had for his soul the entrusting to him of chosen souls: "God has given me an immense spiritual fecundity; souls come to me, and what souls."

Do not think that he helped only those who might be called the "spiritual aristocracy." He gave equal attention to every soul that sought his direction, however lowly it might be. Many a time he wrote to persons whom a simple priest might not have answered, judging them intrusive.

He admits, in all candor, the special graces that God grants him for directing souls. "God has made me aware that my soul needs to be very pure to be able to deal with the many pure souls he has entrusted to me."

Farther on: "Our Lord continues giving me rare gifts for souls. I am frightened at the facility with which I read them even to the depths, at the mastery with which I counsel them. It is not I; it is he."

Are not these the charisms of discernment of spirits and the scrutiny of souls? In another place he states:

The condescension of our Lord is ineffable, for with great solicitude he tells me frequently what he wishes; he warns me against what may not be in due form; he constrains me lest my acts show the least indication of passion, of anything too human, of anything that is not upright and detached. At the same time he gives me light for souls and an efficacy in doing them good. He particularly desires me to do good to priests. It seems to me that each day I identify myself more with souls; their sufferings are my martyrdom; their graces move me and make me happy. The devil has wanted to take some choice souls away from me. He brings me an aversion for counselling, a desire to give up direction, which makes me think that God truly destines me for this ministry and that he works great good through my instrumentality. If worldly eyes were to see these lines, perhaps they would be scandalized.

Our Lord has recently given me the perfect joy of the apostolate; souls give me so much joy, and suffering, too, though incomparably less. I have often felt a strength for supporting and consoling souls as if I apparently needed neither support nor consolation myself. Our Lord has shown me that he constitutes my strength to support and console, and that I need no other than he, so intimately united with my soul. On certain occasions I feel neither the sweetness nor the fervor of union, but peace, strength and an indescribable solidity and intimacy which give testimony to me of that most blessed union.

Some future day Archbishop Martínez' abundant correspondence of direction will be published; a whole practical treatise on spiritual direction can be drawn from it. Meanwhile, let us point out some of the basic principles he followed in exercising this ministry.

1) The true director of souls is the Holy Spirit. The priest is only his instrument. Therefore, he should not take a strictly personal initiative nor point out to souls their way as it appears to him. His role consists only in discerning and seconding the action of the Holy Spirit.

2) At the base of the edifice of supernatural perfection must be placed veracity, rectitude, frankness, loyalty and other natural virtues. Souls refractory to these virtues will not be able to reach perfection, neither are they capable of being directed.

3) He insisted strongly that one must not hurt souls, neither one's own nor another's. In our soul there is something of ourselves and something of God, something mundane and something divine. The divine element is most delicate, like a breath of God, and it deserves gentleness and respect; the earthly element we may despise and abhor, but without forgetting that it is joined with the divine.

"One must not pull out the weeds ruthlessly lest he also pull out the wheat." Through failure to recognize this, directors deform many souls; they want to pluck out the bad without discretion, without gentleness, without tact, so the good is plucked out, too, and the soul is wounded.

We can be energetic, direct, even holily cruel with souls—beginning with our own—but with never-failing sweetness and gentleness. In *substance,* let us not have any consideration: let us pull out, let us cut the root, let us burn; but in *method,* let us be gentle, so as not to pluck out the wheat too.

The method not only signifies the *manner,* in which affability dominates, but the *procedure,* which must not be precipitate, cutting without rhyme or reason, but rather, developing leisurely, orderly, patiently. Patience with ourselves is more difficult and perhaps more necessary than patience with others.

Gentleness is manifested especially in respect to laws imposed on us by God. One of these laws is that reforms in souls come from above, downward, that is, from the conviction of the understanding and from the love of the will. Gentleness is not opposed to strength. One who has slight muscular strength moves a piece of furniture by shoving with might and main; a strong person moves it with ease. Natural forces are very strong and very gentle; and God, the supreme force, is also the supreme gentleness.

One should not stop the flight of souls, but carry them to the heights, to the summits of love and sacrifice, but gently.

4) This brings us to the fourth principle. The Archbishop insisted that virtues are the offspring of light, and they should be practiced through conviction and love. For example, there are those who want humility to be acquired, not through its foundation, which is self-knowledge, but with external beatings and sometimes even with deceit. How many times a person is told that he is foolish to humble himself, since he is not truly humble; that such or such a thing was wrong, when in reality it was not so.

With there proceedings, souls are deformed, because they either believe or do not believe what is said to them. If they do not believe, seeds of hypocrisy and duplicity are sown; if they do believe, by making efforts to subject their judgment they finally lose the criterion for distinguishing good from evil, truth from error. Souls must be trained with truth and influenced with love and gentleness. Under such treatment souls will go to any lengths, to sacrifice, to crucifixion, or at least, they will not be injured.

The more clearly we see, in God's light, his greatness, perfection, and sanctity, the more evident appears our nothingness. Then humility comes forth naturally, as it were. And it is a humility that does not cramp, nor discourage, nor depress, but on the contrary, it invigorates, encourages and moves us to undertake great things.

But when one wants to obtain humility, not through God's light, but by the force of blows, he runs the danger of placing himself outside the truth, making with the worst kind of logic this deduction: I can do nothing by myself, therefore I can do nothing. The divinely logical deduction is this: I can do nothing by myself, therefore I can do everything in God, as St. Paul said: *Cum infirmor, tunc potens sum!* When I feel all my misery, then I am powerful.

5) The Archbishop also placed great emphasis on prayer, in respect to which he had these personal viewpoints.

a) Prayer is not a means to reform our life, but on the contrary, we reform our life to improve our prayer. This does not detract from the fact that prayer has a most powerful influence in the reform of our life.

b) Not only should definite times be set apart for prayer, but it should fill our entire life; we must live a life of prayer, always maintaining the soul in a supernatural atmosphere, seeing all things with the eyes of faith and from the point of view of charity.

c) The more prayer is simplified, the more it is perfected. To a soul that felt an attraction for silent recollection in prayer, and who feared that this might be laziness, he said: "Foster that attraction which you think is laziness; fix your eyes and your heart on the Holy Eucharist and leave yourself to him. It is well to allow him to act, to permit him to do everything, especially in prayer.

6) He insisted especially upon trust and love. He knew so well how to open up broad horizons to souls. He was adept in infusing a living faith whereby souls might believe that God

loved them. When he spoke about God's love, how impassioned his words, how animated his countenance, how transformed his person!

I assure you in the name of Jesus that he loves you with predilection, that he desires you to let your love for him expand fully, and that he wishes to work marvels in your soul, provided that you believe fully in his love.

You may think what you like about your soul, say frightful things about it; but if you believe in Jesus' love, you will understand that this merciful love can make a saint, and he desires to make a saint of that good-for-nothing soul.

And I wonder if that soul might see that it is precisely because it is good for nothing that Jesus loves it surpassingly and has singular designs upon it?

Jesus has very strange taste and even quite spiritual persons do not know it. For my part, I hold that one of the greatest graces that he has given me has been to discover for myself his taste, because by knowing "his weak side," one can do with him what one wants.

I do not then set about discussing your miseries with you except to support myself upon them to say to you: Jesus loves you tremendously and he wishes to build prodigies of mercy upon your wretchedness.

To destroy your disillusion of yourself I give you only one means: to believe in the love of Jesus, to be penetrated each moment with that love. To think and feel that Jesus loves you may seem to you ridiculous, foolhardy, illusory; embrace the ridiculous, the foolhardy, the illusory,—do you know why?—to be embraced by truth.

Does it not seem an ingratitude, a deceit, almost a cruelty, to have passed so many years without understanding Jesus, unmindful of his intimate affection, without realizing the predilection which he has shown you and without thanking him for it?

Who does not understand that such spiritual direction developed souls, making them fly toward union with God through love? But his direction consisted not only in guiding souls but in praying for them. For example, he writes in his notes: "A soul of election was undergoing intense suffering and on June 21 I said to God that through his love for me would he give it respite; and at once the sufferings were changed into tender consolations."

And in another place:

On St. Augustine's day I preached for the fifteenth centenary of the saint. In the sermon I stated that St. Augustine tended toward contemplation through all the attractions of his soul, and that, in my judgment, he had accepted the active life as a cross.

I confess that upon saying it, I felt that way myself. Well then, shortly afterwards, our Lady taught me a prayer that I never heard of; you might call it *prayer of the active life*. During it I occupied myself neither with God nor myself, but with souls, presenting them to the Lord with their necessities and their virtues, and making petition for them with an earnestness unknown till then. But the noteworthy thing is that my soul found therein such rest, such sweetness, as if I were occupying myself with contemplation of God loving him.

The following day, I made my prayer again in the same way, now purposely; since the first time it was not a thing thought out beforehand, but the impulse came upon me suddenly.

The second time, the same holy affection came; I ran over the series of souls that for one reason or other are intertwined with mine, and I noted God's complacency in that.

On another occasion he states that on a certain date God gave a very special grace to a soul under his direction. He rejoices as if he himself had received it, and he writes:

I helped this soul, sustaining it in trials and preparing it for union. That very day, during the night—during the day I was very busy—our Lord made me share in the feast, uniting himself with me intimately and rapturously as never before. He calmed me lovingly and kindly, giving me heavenly moments in the solitude of my oratory.

At midnight, I had to tear myself away from there to sleep. I believed that was all and in truth it was superabundant; but no, it continued the whole octave and days afterwards, with very close union, celestial consolations and glorious lights.

Under such a director, it is very clear that souls reached sanctity, if they corresponded with the grace of God. For example, Monsignor Rafael Guiza opened his soul to Archbishop Martínez with the simplicity of a child. His process of beatification is now in progress in Rome.

We must mention also Señora Concepción Cabrera de Armida, whom he directed from early July in 1924 to her death on March 3, 1937. No doubt she had other directors before, but certainly no one guided her so well as His Excellency, no one opened up such broad horizons, no one understood her soul so thoroughly, no one inspired her with such determination for her sanctification.

The correspondence which he kept up with her and the retreats which he preached to her each year could form several volumes, not to mention personal interviews. When her last illness came, he would hasten at her summons, wherever he might be. Once, summoned at a late hour from Monterrey, he travelled all night by automobile, arriving in Mexico at dawn. The last time, they called him from Morelia; he travelled all night and, drenched with rain and covered with mud, he arrived in Mexico City at three in the morning.[8]

He had the consolation of assisting her in her agony and of delivering to the Lord this beloved soul for whom he had sacrificed so much. A few months before his death, he had the satisfaction of issuing a decree to initiate the process of her beatification.

The Archbishop could well say of those souls, who must

[8] A little after midnight, the auto stalled in the mud. The Archbishop and Canon Buitrón, who accompanied him, had to get out to push the car. As the wheels kept revolving on the same spot, they were sprinkled with mud from head to foot.

have come out to meet him at his entrance into heaven, "You are my joy and my crown."

The apostolate of Archbishop Martínez was manifested, as we have seen, by the formation of holy souls, and the preaching of the sacred word, spoken or written; but there was a multitude of other manifestations. We shall limit ourselves to his nineteen years' government of the Archdiocese of Mexico.

His first preoccupation, upon taking charge, was the seminary. More than decimated by the recent persecutions, despoiled of its beautiful building, it had been forced to take refuge partly in Temascalcingo, partly in the annex of the parish of Tlalpan. That seminary, with so glorious a past, with a century of traditions, needed a true resurrection.

The task was manifold: to seek and select good vocations, to multiply them; to select and augment the teaching personnel; to intensify the spiritual and intellectual formation; to extend the program of studies and to provide the seminary with a new building.

His Excellency succeeded in constructing a magnificent building in colonial style with a magnificent facade, spacious cloisters and halls, individual rooms and other features. The chapel was left to the end and is still being completed.

Desirous of attending to the seminary personally, he retained for several years the burden of rector until in 1953 he named one of his auxiliaries to that position. Many times he preached spiritual retreats to his seminarians, and in the thirty-two years of his episcopate, the priests he ordained are innumerable; moreover, he consecrated ten bishops.

If he strove for the formation of his seminarians, with greater reason and determination he devoted himself to the sanctification of his priests, especially through the practice of the spiritual exercises which he himself frequently preached.

Another colossal work was the reconstruction of the cathedral. Because of the instability of the subsoil in the valley of

Mexico, the cathedral was sinking and splitting; the wood floor was in very bad condition, as was proven by its collapse on the very day His Excellency took possession of the archdiocese. It was necessary to lay anew the foundation of the cathedral.

In addition to the foundation, a huge crypt was constructed for burial places, with a special one, under the altar of the Kings, for the prelates of the archdiocese. During the lifetime of Archbishop Martínez, the remains of five prelates were transferred there, among them the first and the last: Fray Juan de Zumárraga and Archbishop Pascual Díaz.

The new floor of the cathedral was made of marble and, given the great dimensions of this church, the largest in Latin America. We can imagine its cost. The arches were girded in order to avoid another collapse, the old main altar was removed.

Archbishop Martínez always was distinguished by his devotion to the most holy Virgin of Guadalupe, and without doubt, God willed that as a recompense her image would remain under his custody, as successor of Fray Juan de Zumárraga. The Archbishop did not content himself with this honor, but he worked with great determination to finish the work of restoration of the Basilica begun by his predecessor, Archbishop Díaz. The abbot, His Excellency Felicián Cortés, also played an important part in this undertaking.

On the feast day, October 12, the Archbishop presented the new Basilica to the most holy Virgin with these touching words:

Holy Mary of Guadalupe, Queen of Mexico! In the name of the episcopate, the clergy and the Mexican people—your people by predilection—I now solemnly offer to you the magnificent basilica that your children have completed for you with such perfection.

This is the homage of our sincere faith, of our profound veneration, of our immense love. Look at it, Mother, and accept it in your gracious way!

This is the church that you asked of Juan Diego, that has been under construction for four centuries. All generations have placed their hands upon it and their hearts within. We have placed our hands and our hearts here also. Lady, our work is finished! Your desires are fulfilled! Your will is accomplished!

Look at it, Mother! Human eyes cannot see all its beauty, but your maternal eyes read the history of each hewn stone, each arch, each column, each moulding; your maternal eyes discover in this temple something mysterious and exquisite: the sacrifice with which it has been adorned in your honor! We made it in difficult epochs marked by scarcity of resources and bitter difficulties. Therefore, it is so beautiful in your eyes and so pleasing to your heart.

Now then, with holy audacity, my Mother, I say to you at this moment what I dare to say only to you: Repay us! You promised Juan Diego that in gratitude you would pay with celestial munificence all that might be done to fulfill your request. Lady, we have concluded our work; we wish to receive the recompense from your blessed hands!

To speak of pay would be a niggardly thing if I did not know that you, my Mother, had first desired ardently to pay us for the little or the much that we might do for you.

Lady, the pay that I presume to specify is the immediate realization of that other desire of your heart which you manifested on the hill of Tepeyac. You asked for a temple. It is made. But in your maternal heart you were thinking about another temple, a spiritual edifice that would extend over the vastness of our continent, formed by the hearts of all your children, a temple in which Jesus Christ would be King and you would be Lady and Queen: a temple of peace, of liberty, of love.

Mother, may that be our reward. In return for this material temple, give us the other. And give it to us soon, for the glory of God, for your honor and for the good of your children. Then on that tomorrow, O our Lady and our Queen, when we celebrate the dedication of the spiritual temple, the immense temple of souls, may there resound throughout our whole vast land the new Canticle, the glorious Canticle: "He has not done thus to every nation!"

The Archbishop then undertook the construction of an immense plaza in front of the Basilica, the "Plaza of the Americas," which could accommodate the great multitudes for whom the Basilica was inadequate. The platform would have a large portico, two monuments, one of Fray Juan de Zumárraga and another of Juan Diego, and two gardens at the sides. Moreover, a new market would be built to replace the unsightly stalls surrounding the Basilica. In 1954, in observance of his sacerdotal jubilee, Archbishop Martínez, now almost on the eve of leaving this world, had the consolation of inaugurating these projects.

It also fell to the lot of Archbishop Martínez to celebrate the fiftieth anniversary of the coronation of Our Lady of Guadalupe on October 12, 1945, in a solemnity without precedent. It was prepared throughout an entire Jubilee Year, in which were held Eucharistic Congresses and local Guadalupan Congresses. The Pontifical Legate, Cardinal Villeneuve, invited by Archbishop Martínez, came to the festivity itself, as well as sixty-eight bishops, innumerable priests and pilgrims from a great part of the continent.

To help us realize that these works were the external fruit of his love for the most holy Virgin, let us quote some paragraphs from his personal notes.

There came to my soul the remembrance of what I saw and felt the day of the imposition of the pallium.[9] I do not doubt that Mary most holy communicated with me; with clearest lights and interior impressions, she offered to me *mine*,—I know the meaning very well—but in exchange for my attending holily to the interests

[9] Archbishop Leopoldo Ruiz invested Archbishop Martínez with the pallium in the Basilica of Guadalupe.

of this diocese and insofar as it concerns me, of the whole Republic, for they are very dear to her.

It is impossible to attend to those interests, if Jesus does not live in me. Nor did I accept it, except on condition that he live in me.

October 11. Today I attended Morelia's ceremony in the Basilica of Guadalupe, and I had delightful moments, near Mary's lovely image and the altar upon which Jesus was immolated. Love and admiration for the most holy Virgin have increased. Today I feel united to her; and through her, united to Jesus. What more can one desire? And I thought about my diocese and that of Morelia, but especially about the entire Mexican nation.

October 12. I pontificated in the Basilica. Jesus manifested himself as very pleased. When I began the Mass, the holy Virgin filled me with consolation. I could not help but weep. I have not felt maternal tenderness for a long time!

On the feast of Our Lady of Sorrows, I experienced an enrichment of deep devotion to Mary, not only because I know that to her I owe all my spiritual good, but because I saw clearly that she teaches me to know Jesus, to love him, to deal with him, to give him pleasure; for no one has known and loved him, given him pleasure and dealt with him as she. Besides, she can show me the shade of love that suits me. With her as teacher and as mother, what sweet intimacy with Jesus, what a heaven on earth!

The most noteworthy thing in my soul these days has been the heavenly impression that possessed it in the Guadalupan celebrations, as if Mary most holy had communicated with me and given me to Jesus in an ineffable manner.

Yesterday, November 1, when I had to go to the Basilica to sing a *Te Deum,* I scarcely saw the dear image of most holy Mary of Guadalupe; then I again felt her presence and I shed tears."

Although Mexico City was the first archdiocese established in Mexico, after more than four centuries it fell to the lot of Archbishop Martínez to hold the first Synod in April, 1945. Very wise regulations were decreed in 413 articles, and several appendices in a volume of 526 pages.

It was difficult to visit the entire archdiocese, not only on account of its extent and the difficulty of transportation in some places, but especially on account of the constant political commotions and the religious persecutions that have filled almost all this century. Archbishop Martínez achieved the visitation of his entire archdiocese, even the most remote places. As he sought nothing but the greater good of souls, he graciously accepted the division of his diocese, already dismembered several times to form others, to form the diocese of Toluca, in spite of the fact that in that region the best vocations for the seminary were found.

It is not difficult to imagine all the labor entailed by the pastoral visit, in which it is necessary not only to deal with all kinds of matters, but also to preach, to confirm, to hear confessions, and perform other pastoral functions.

The greatest number of religious communities in the entire nation is in the Archdiocese of Mexico. The Archbishop, who appreciated so greatly the religious life, who had confidence in the prayers of the contemplative communities and in the cooperation of the active communities, was vigilant for their spiritual formation. He desired that the vicar of religious, who represented him, would be, whenever possible, a religious, so that knowing the religious life through his own experience, he could take care of the religious more efficiently. To him he entrusted their spiritual formation, above all else. The Archbishop personally accepted the invitations of communities to preach the exercises and retreats, and to preside at the clothing and profession ceremonies.

But he was watchful not only of the spiritual formation, but also of the professional education of religious teachers. In order to give more attention to matters relative to teaching, he appointed as his representative for this purpose a priest of the Society of Jesus, as experienced as prudent. Anxious about the education of poor girls and boys, he insisted that high schools for the upper social classes have in addition a free school for the poor. He was not unmindful, either, of secular teachers. He organized a select group from their number and with special solicitude he used to give them personally a monthly retreat, until his strength failed him.

Archbishop Martínez came from Morelia, which at the present time is perhaps the center where sacred music is best organized in the entire country. Upon arriving in Mexico, in the midst of such great preoccupations, he was not unmindful of this matter, which he believed had great importance, since it forms part of the sacred liturgy, of the worship due to God. For this purpose, he established the Diocesan Council of Sacred Music, he issued rules and regulations upon the material itself, and struggling with great difficulties and finally conquering them, he founded the School of Sacred Music.

Although man does not live by bread alone, we must not on that account be careless about economic matters. The Church lives on tithes; but as a consequence of political disturbances, agriculture had deteriorated greatly and therefore the tithes were very small. So the Archbishop, after considering the matter for several years, organized the tithes in another form, so that all the faithful could contribute in one form or another to the support of the Church. He endeavored not to make it a burden, and he authorized the pastors to make concessions and give necessary dispensations.

It would be interminable to continue enumerating the works he carried to completion: the organizations of workmen and farmers, the social works, the establishment of the catechetical office, the numerous parishes that he founded, the new churches that were constructed under his government, the modern organization of the offices of the curia, and many other undertakings. But perhaps one of his most surpassing exterior accomplishments was his work as pacifier. He arrived in Mexico City in truly difficult times. The relations between the two governments, civil and religious, were undergoing a deplorable strain. His predecessor, Archbishop Díaz, who is rightly called Mexico's martyr archbishop, was undoubtedly the victim of this tension. Archbishop Martínez came to Mexico City like the dove from the ark; even more, like Christ who came to bring us peace. This undertaking was not something casual; in his spiritual exercises we frequently find this resolution repeated from the first retreat that he made as archbishop.

To carry out the work of unity and harmony, "that all may be one," was Jesus' desire on the night of his Passion. It is without doubt his constant desire regarding the Church and especially in Mexico.

Union with God, with the Holy See, with the episcopate. Union among the priests. Union among the faithful. Union with the government as far as possible and fitting.

This was his program, a program he announced in his first Pastoral Letter, all of it consecrated to peace, and in his first greeting to his bishops: "Peace be to you." In order to accomplish his work of pacification, he employed only supernatural means.

It is the same in the mystery of the Redemption as in the salvation of each soul and the salvation of each people; there are those who think that signs of glory and power are necessary, and even those who judge that human sagacity and prudence can save. In reality, the only salvation for souls and for peoples is Jesus Crucified, not only as a source of grace, but as a model to emulate; or rather, we must incorporate ourselves with him in order to share in his mysteries and especially in his sacrifice.

When on February 14, 1937, the Holy See asked his consent to his appointment as Archbishop of Mexico City, he made a pact with our Lord which he called the pact of San Antonio, because of the city in which it took place: San Antonio, Texas. He told our Lord that he accepted, on condition that he would bind himself to do it all, so that the archbishop would be only an instrument: "that you speak through my lips, work with my activity, and govern by using me."

Throughout his episcopate he proved at each step that our Lord complied with the pact of San Antonio:

My burdens are a stimulus to live united to Jesus, for if he would forsake me, my failure would be complete and how many souls and how many sacred interests would be lost! And in proportion to my union with Jesus, will be the fruitfulness of my life and the success of my pastoral works.

I ought to live the life of Jesus and live it in its entirety, because my heart asks for it. My burdens demand it imperiously. God has given me a vast, important, difficult Church; the year that I have passed here makes me see the magnitude of the task and the terrible responsibilities that it has imposed upon me. On the other hand, representing the Holy See broadens my field of action and expands enormously my responsibility. How much good I can do if I am what I ought to be! How much evil, if I am not!

And in a letter:

Do you remember the "pact of San Antonio?" When I accepted this archbishopric, I placed upon our Lord a condition that he would have to do everything and that I would be his megaphone and instrument. He has complied very well; and sometimes, when I see myself hurried, I recall the pact.

But the past month (May, 1941) it occurred to me—perhaps he inspired me—that this contract is imperfect, if it is understood as unilateral, that is, as if the whole agreement were on his part and I do nothing on my part but the "Yes" of February 14, 1937. For the perfection of the agreement, I ought to be his instrument; so that I do my best in the fulfillment of my duty, to do his will, and not only in the sense that I place what is proper on my part for success, but principally in the sense that, if he has given me as much in the general mission as in particular cases, he may manifest his will to me whether I do such a thing or pursue such a course. Through fidelity to the pact, I ought to fulfill his designs the best that I possibly can; for the entire agreement brings with it mutual rights and obligations.

As on that occasion he was in the same place in which he had originally made the pact—the chapel of the Incarnate Word in San Antonio—he renewed it in the form mentioned above.

Yesterday a person said to me nothing less than this: "I do not envy you your little burden," alluding to the difficulties and sufferings that my responsibility brings with it. But I thought: "He does not know the peace in which I live!" For I know that Jesus arranges it all, he does all for me; and this security makes me confident.

In this last season, I have had, or rather, I have lived, those words of St. Paul: "Everything, and in everything, Christ." I feel that he is the source of all my activity: he speaks, he works in me; he preaches, he directs, he governs, he decides everything. He arranges for me even the most difficult things. This produces in me a profound peace; it is the cause of my spiritual "indifference."

He wants to be the only one in my desires, my resolutions, my intentions. I ought to seek nothing but his interests. That was the characteristic of my Holy Week and of my Easter: *to forget myself and everything,* to think only about him, about his sorrows and his joys, his humiliations and his triumphs, his interests and his life. As for the rest and my own self, I want to see all in him, to love it in him.

And even in each one of my acts, he should be all: to love him, to give him, to promote his glory, to make all, as a mathematician would say, a *function* of Jesus.

A short time ago they told me that I am very fortunate, that I was born to good luck. It is true, but the secret of that luck is that Jesus does everything for me. I have noticed that when I want to excell through my own management, things do not turn out so well as when I let myself be guided by him.

I have many and very difficult problems, but they do not worry me because I am not alone, I am with Jesus and he counsels me, he arranges all for me, I confide in him. I live with him, I feel his love and I give him mine, poor but sincere.

Lately he has made me see the deficiencies in my love and he has made me very ashamed of corresponding so poorly to his ineffable goodness. I still have not finished with the task of forgetting myself, but he has inspired a deep desire to think only about him, of being preoccupied only with his interests, of wanting nothing else than to give him pleasure. Thanks be to God, my time is for Jesus and all my occupations bear a relation to him.

In former retreats I stated my problem thus: In order to fulfill my very serious obligations I need an intense interior life, a deep, solid love. Now the statement is reversed: I ought to have a deep, absorbing love in my soul; the fulfillment of my pastoral duties is but the logical consequence of my love.

More than to discharge my obligations properly, more than to have a fruitful apostolate, I need a deep love, a love that may fill my heart and my life. Now here are the *revelations:*[10]

1) The *singular* love, the predilection that Jesus has had for me, is the key of my life and of my destiny.

2) The key of that predilection of Jesus is the predilection of Mary, to whom my parents consecrated me before I was born.

3) Jesus gave me the assurance of my union with him; the graces of 1927 are a sweet, living reality.

4) The apostolic life is love, fruitful love which reproduces Jesus. This revelation refers to the special color of my love. There is a love that *seeks* the beloved everywhere. There is another, mine, which *reproduces* Jesus everywhere. This revelation refers to the special color of my love.

5) Divine love has all the charms, all the characteristics, all the exigencies of human love; naturally all this is increased and surpassed.

I had a delightful month of June. Jesus filled me with light and comfort. The principal thing was the transformation. I am to do *only* the work of Jesus, to watch over his interests, to accomplish his designs, and to count upon him, his light, his direction and his strength for everything. How keenly I experience his working in me, his guiding me! All his, mine; all mine, his.

[10] The term "revelations" refers not to private revelations but to special lights upon truths already commonly known.

I have the impression that the Holy Spirit possesses my soul; but the principal effect of that possession is to *concentrate my heart and my life upon Jesus.*

To love him, with a shade that I dare not speak of . . ; to look at him, to serve him, to sacrifice all for him. Naturally this impression is accompanied by a deep recollection that seizes the soul without restraining or thwarting it.

No one can imagine the problems that I have at each instant. Necessity and experience oblige me to rest in him; I leave all to him and he arranges it all for me.

This Easter season has been for me a time of lights and consolations. Jesus has *fondled* me, although I have not responded as I ought to his tenderness. During the ceremonies I attended and especially during very delightful nights near the tabernacle, our Lord made me feel his love and his union.

I have felt three things principally: a great confidence that he will manage everything and solve my problems, a most intense adherence to his holy will in whatever he wishes to send me, and a need of treating with him in complete intimacy and of uniting myself with him.

This idea has dominated me: that Jesus do my work, and that I do the work of Jesus! This is my constant petition in the quick visits that I make to the Blessed Sacrament almost each time that I leave the house or that I begin some important work.

The first part of this petition I already explained in regard to the pact of San Antonio; it is necessary that he govern, exhort, preach, and do other duties through me. Thus everything will come out well, and I shall live in peace and confidence. On many occasions I have noticed his influence clearly.

But in order that he do my work, it is necessary that I do his, that is, there are not two tasks, but one, his. To do his work, I need to do his will constantly, to give him pleasure in everything, in great things and in small.

Some times unexpectedly I feel his presence and his action. It seems to me that he does it to show me his pleasure for something I did or to attract me when I wander.

I am never alone. I rely upon him. Has he not discharged my duties? Does he not protect me unceasingly? And especially, do I not love him in my tabernacle and in my heart? He is my counsellor and my friend, he is something more; he is my all. How sweet it is to rest in Jesus, to depend fully upon him!

I also am all for Jesus; in spite of the deficiencies of my smallness, I do his work as he does mine. Mine and his are the same work, because we are ineffably united.

A short time ago this delightful idea came to me. I had yielded two satisfactions in cases where I saw his preference. One of these is closely connected with my duties. My thought placed him above these satisfactions. However important my duties be, however urgent my occupations, the supreme thing, for me, the only thing, is the love of Jesus, our mutual love. Yes, my duties, my occupations are something superficial and secondary; the profound, the essential thing is my union with Jesus. Oh, truly, we are the one for the other!

The Archbishop used to say that the means which he employed were supernatural, especially prayer and sacrifices. But there is no doubt that he had also qualities and virtues which fitted him for this work. He possessed, of course, rectitude and loyalty, sincerity and fidelity. In him there was nothing confused, crooked; his intention was always upright, his attitude candid and definite, he held all diplomacy in horror; his great diplomacy was not to have any. "To keep me *in the truth*. This involves sincerity, logic and rectitude. 'Sanctify them in truth'."

In his subject matter for the retreats he insisted at each step upon prudence. In him it was not the simple virtue of prudence, but the gift of counsel; therefore, Monsignor Ruiz Solórzano who knew him thoroughly, says of him: "I have the impression that more than Archbishop of Mexico City he was the guide of the Church in Mexico; his mission was rather a national mission." And that national mission was, as we have been saying, a mission of peace and of union; to this end he sacrificed everything.

Much was said of his elevation to the cardinalate. We do not exaggerate in saying that in the mind of everyone, from the Supreme Pontiff to the last Mexican, none was so worthy of this honor. Since cardinals were named in all countries except Mexico, even behind the Iron Curtain, some Mexicans wondered at this and even took a certain scandal, not only because of the merits of Archbishop Martínez, but because it seemed that thirty million Mexican Catholics should have a representative in the elections of the Supreme Pontiff. Moreover, had not Mexican blood been shed for the faith?

Some explained this seeming anomaly by saying that diplomatic relations were needed with the Holy See, but that the laws of Mexico were opposed to the Church and would place the dignity of a cardinal in danger.

Nevertheless, the true reason is this: when Cardinal Villeneuve came to Mexico, he realized from the enthusiastic faith of the Mexican people, from their devotion to the Pope, and from the merits of Archbishop Martínez, that he should be a cardinal. A short time afterwards, he went to Rome and although it is not possible to ascertain it with scientific certitude, everything leads us to conjecture that, upon giving an account to the Holy Father of his mission as Papal Legate, he discussed this affair, because after his return to Quebec, he wrote to Archbishop Martínez and asked His Excellency to say whether it would be opportune to name a cardinal in Mexico.

Archbishop Martínez held very lofty views and he moved on a high supernatural plane. He commanded me to answer Cardinal Villeneuve's letter in these terms: the naming of a cardinal in Mexico was not opportune, because it could be a cause for disturbance by the enemies of the Church. Given the impetuous temperament of the Mexicans, the creation of a cardinal would create a sensation, it would attract the attention of the enemies of the Church and could produce a reaction that would destroy the peace obtained with such great efforts.

Everybody understood; it did not escape Archbishop Martínez himself if a cardinal were named it would be he; but he sacrificed it all to maintain peace and union.

CHAPTER VII

Apostle Of Love

WE HAVE SEEN something of the spirituality of Archbishop Martínez, which he attributed to the grace that he received on September 27, 1927. But we can clarify it further by making known the mission which our Lord entrusted to him. This mission was revealed to him a little at a time. In his later years he understood it clearly, as he shows in his personal notes.[1]

It had perfect unity or, if you wish, it was a mission that manifested itself in three ways:

1) To be an apostle of the love of Jesus.
2) To be a living portrait of Jesus.
3) To be a victim with Jesus.

Let us speak briefly of each of these.

In his innumerable sermons; in the exercises and retreats

---

[1] "I have been preoccupied lately with the missions that God has pointed out to me. Each day I see them with greater clarity; this both pleases and embarrasses me. It pleases me because those missions are lofty and beautiful; it embarrasses me because they seem too lofty and beautiful for my misery.

"The day on which I came from Teziutlán to Mexico City (August 4, 1941) I was alone for four hours and I had time to reflect upon those missions.

"I had not thought seriously about it (however well I know that every soul coming into this world has some mission) or I had thought that it was some fragmentary, passing work for which our Lord made use of me.

"Now I see clearly that Jesus desires to show in me how love accomplishes the mystery of God doing a divine work through a miserable being."

(Of the second mission he speaks in another place, as we shall see.)

"I see in the third mission—to be a victim with Jesus—the interlocking of my soul with the 'Works of the Cross'."

that he preached, especially to religious; in his extensive correspondence for spiritual direction; in all his works, published and unpublished, the one theme is *love:* the love of Jesus for the soul or the love of the soul for Jesus. Sometimes he treats it in an indirect manner, more or less veiled; again, he speaks clearly about it, from an overflowing heart. This was also the theme of his own annual spiritual exercises. In one word, this was the obsession of his life.

If we were to quote all his private notes that pertain to the love of Jesus, it would be necessary to cite almost all of them and, consequently, we would never finish. Nevertheless, let us select some quotations at random.

In his retreat of 1936, he writes:

Days with Jesus. May he fill, as I want him to fill, my heart and my life and my eternity. I think that he wants these days and that he will be happy, because he loves me and he has asked me for them. What attracts me most is intimacy with Jesus; I feel it and I desire it; I thirst for it. I should like him to lay open to me his secrets, especially the secrets of his beauty and his love.

For some days I feel myself in intimate communication with him, heart to heart; he can say to me what he wishes to say, or rather, I can read in his heart what he wishes to say to me.

They tell me that Jesus is pleased with me: he himself seems to confirm this welcome news. I am happy, not because I am perfect, but because he looks at me with eyes of mercy. One would say that those eyes do not see my imperfections but only my heart.

I was created for Jesus by an eternal predilection. I belong to him. I was created to love him, to be eternally his, to serve him, to share in his suffering. He is the reason of my being. What happiness to be his own possession, to be nothing but something belonging to him! From all eternity I have belonged to him and I hope by his mercy to belong to him for all eternity. As perfume belongs to the flower, as foam to the waters, as stars to the firmament, so I belong to Jesus.

My belonging is *total.* Everything in me is his, my being, my life, my eternity. The thoughts of my soul, the beatings of my heart, the moments of my life are his, his by every right, completely his. Nothing of mine can detract from his sovereignty without injustice, ingratitude and offense to love.

To be completely his, to be possessed fully by him is my perfection and my happiness. My whole spiritual life ought to tend toward belonging totally to Jesus. Jesus must be the sovereign of my heart. May his victorious love fill it, penetrate it, absorb it, without leaving a single fiber untouched. He must be the sovereign of my activity and of my life. To accomplish this most delightful work, it is necessary that Jesus captivate my heart. Love is not the work of reasoning but a mystery of powerful attraction. The heart does not yield to the number and forces of reasons but to the radiance and the irresistible sight of the Beloved.

O Jesus, reveal yourself to my soul; show me your face and let your voice sound in my ears! So many veils cover you from my eyes: the canopy, the tabernacle, the ciborium, the Eucharistic species. Through all these veils I discern your most sacred humanity, full of charm, of majesty, of beauty, of harmony. I perceive that this marvel is only the precious jewel that incloses the unspeakable treasure of the divinity that penetrates it and fills it with God's own plenitude.

The only thing that can captivate and subdue our poor human heart is the divinity; the heart was made for God; the heart is the void, the capacity, the aspiration for God. If creatures allure and attract it, it is on account of the divine reflection within them.

The names that we give to all things that our heart desires are fragmentary formulas expressing something divine. They try to delineate a facet of the divine reality. Glory, wealth, love, happiness, either are God or they are fleeting illusions. God is glory, God is wealth, God is love, God is felicity. When the soul comes to perceive this, it surrenders and hands itself over without delay, without compromise, in the fullness of its love, in the sincerity of its giving, in the opulence of its renunciation.

No one gives this heavenly treasure to us in the same way as the sacred humanity of Jesus. He gives it to us with marvelous abundance because in him is the fullness of the Godhead. He gives it to us, adapting it in an unspeakable manner to our smallness. One would say that he screens the "light inaccessible" so that it bathes our soul without dazzling it, without oppressing it with the weight of his majesty. He gives us heavenly treasure as something of our own, with an inexplicable tint of intimacy.

Our brother according to the flesh, Jesus makes us his brother in that which is divine; he introduces us into the bosom of God with the rights of the Word, imparting to us the intimacy of the most beloved Son in whom the Father is well pleased.

Attract me, O Jesus, with that irresistible, profound, victorious attraction with which you draw those blessedly conquered souls to whom you show yourself. "Draw us in the odor of thy ointments."

Such is the theme of all his retreats: belonging to Jesus, the meaning of this belonging and the means to attain it. At the end he says:

The only theme of these exercises was the love of Jesus; and I lived that theme with such effectiveness that at the close I felt renewed in love.

What have you done with me, O Jesus, that I feel enamored of you? My heart, exalted in undimmed brightness, with all obstacles vanished, as it were, I feel far from creatures, yet that distance of purity and of love does not disturb my intimate communication with the souls God has recommended to me. It is similar to the way that Jesus in the Eucharist is near, very near our souls, yet in this wonderful sacrament he is far, very far, from all that is earthly.

Will the holy impressions, the precious effects, the noon-day light of these days pass away? No, I had one confidential hour in particular. I delivered myself to Jesus, I cast myself into his arms and into his heart, and I bound myself to the fulfillment of my resolutions. I said to him: I made them, you fulfill them.

It seems to me that he is keenly interested in the renewal of my spiritual life. His love is as impatient as mine. Beyond a doubt, a new stage in my spiritual life is beginning. Perhaps it is the last. Jesus is preparing me for something. Can it be for death? Can it be for perfect love?

In reality, God was preparing him to be Archbishop of Mexico, for seven months later he was transferred to this new and exceedingly vast field of action. He concludes thus:

During the night, at the foot of my tabernacle, Jesus treated me to a delightful heavenly feast. Just as if all obstacles between us had suddenly disappeared, I flung myself into his arms and he came into my heart. What did Jesus do in my poor heart during these exercises? It is a new heart, perfectly attached to Jesus and welded by a new, ardent, tender, simple, audacious love.

On that heavenly night, he hid neither his pleasure nor his love. He united me with himself, he caressed me, he filled me with light, with his consolations, with his joy. I told him many things with the simplicity of a child, with the ardor of a lover. And he told me without words his secrets of love. I dragged myself away from his side with violence, bearing in my soul his heavenly fragrance.

Some days later, he notes:

Afterwards came the whirlpool of occupations; but I am another person. At first, my soul imbued with heavenly fragrance; later, as was natural, it kept fading away. But, I repeat, I am another person, for I feel alienated from the world, totally attached to Jesus, all for him, free from impediments and eager for the divine intimacy.

Jesus and I continue in communication; at each step he guides me; many times I feel his action, especially the jealous solicitude with which he ingenuously alienates me from all that could attract my heart. He loves me jealously! He intervenes in all that could flatter my self-love, putting some little grain of bitterness or a sparkle from heaven so that nothing may distract me from him. He reprimands me lovingly, he impels me, he seems to have nothing else to do but to care for me.

Rightly did he tell me not to pay attention to obstacles; he takes them away. Rightly did he inspire me to bind myself to fulfill my resolutions; he takes charge of them."

Archbishop Martínez' love for Jesus had some characteristic features. One discerns a special devotion to the mystery of the infancy of Jesus. This made his love simple, ingenuous, candid, childlike, trustful, daring. In brief, his love had all the characteristics of spiritual infancy.

I love Jesus in the style of St. Joseph, which basically is not different from Mary's love. I should like to love him with that tenderness, purity and disinterestedness, with that generosity, that eagerness to enfold him, to care for him and, as it were, to protect him.

That way of loving him seems proper to the priest, for each time that we say Mass or give him to souls, could we not say, like the heavenly Father: "Thou art my Son; this day I have begotten thee"? Throughout the transforming union there are two shades of love, the nuptial and *this one;* because the Word is spouse of the soul and Jesus is the fruit.

His favorite festival was Christmas. On that day he sang his first Mass. Around that feast, he arranged, as far as possible, his annual spiritual exercises "so as to spend those days in the cave of Bethlehem." Let us see some examples:

What a Christmas! Decidedly, this is my feast. I never fail to weep on that night and I never fail to feel it deeply. Not even in my most relaxed times did I fail to experience the sacred emotion of that night.

The following year, through a special delicacy of our Lord, and in spite of many difficulties, he had the happiness of spending that Christmas in Bethlehem and of celebrating Holy Mass there in the very place where Jesus was born. On another date he writes:

I have noticed that my love is taking a tinge of simplicity, of trust, like a child: a child at fifty years of age! But souls are not ruled in everything by time. Love is the youth of the soul, and that same youth is sometimes tinged with the dawn-like glow of childhood.

I do not come near explaining what that tint of love means to me. It has the shade of a very intimate trust, for however great the trust an adult may have in the one he loves, that confidence necessarily has its limitations, while that of the child is limitless.

There are certain affairs in which older persons ask help of those they love, through confidence, through love; but the child, on similar occasions, does not ask help in the same way; he asks help from his mother or whoever takes care of him as if that person had an obligation to help him.

And it is so in reality; to dress the child, however personal a matter it may be, is not his responsibility but his mother's. The union of the child with his mother is closer than the union of two older persons who love each other; there is between the first a greater union of interests and a greater, a much greater trust. In the other case, that affection has such intimacy, such depth, such abandonment, that the union is accordingly closer, easier, sweeter. And the tinge of innocence, of candor. . . ?"

Another year he wrote:

My Advent was extraordinary, redolent with my grace of September 21, and consequently by a remote but lovely analogy, of the Advent of the Blessed Virgin.

On the other hand, my Christmas did not have the sensible pomp of other years. I spent it in Abasolo and I celebrated the Midnight Mass in silence, in a narrow room. The sermon that I preached that day for some silver sacerdotal jubilees was but a slight outlet for my deep sentiments. The theme was this: Jesus is always being born in the Church and in the priests. Both nativities have the perenniality of a spring that does not fade away, of an interior youth that is eternal.

Another year he writes:

I do not need much to make me feel the joy of Bethlehem on Christmas night. It is my feast. Consolation never fails me on that night and each year the impression seems to be new and more intense.

I asked the Child as a Christmas gift that a law already prepared might not be imposed, for it would bring disturbance to the schools. Soon I understood that he would not grant it to me, but my soul, far from being disturbed, was filled with joy upon adhering to his will, not only because it is wise and loving, but because it is from him.

Little by little the sensible impression keeps vanishing but the spiritual stays on. I feel my soul lovingly pledged to Jesus. Having him in the tabernacle and in my heart, neither anything nor anyone can take away joy and happiness. As the author of the *Imitation* said: "To be with Jesus is a sweet paradise."

My Christmas desire is that my new surrender to Jesus be full and definitive. How many reserves and how many deficiencies in our surrenders! Twenty-five years of copious graces have not been long enough to make Jesus the complete gift of myself. May he grant me to celebrate that happy anniversary by offering him that gift in a definitive way.

On the following Christmas he comments:

I began Advent in a Pullman car and there I learned, in God's own way of speaking, that during the new ecclesiastical year I ought to cultivate the love of Jesus with the shade that is proper to me; that I have not exploited as much as I ought the spiritual favor of 1927, and that therefore my Advent should be directed toward that end. What marvelous models Mary and Joseph are for pursuing that end! How they disposed themselves for the happiness of Bethlehem! What purity! What desire! What unity of intention in all their works!"

For the second Sunday in Advent, which coincides with the feast of the Immaculate Conception, I received a new light coming in a distinctive manner from the hands of Mary. It can be expressed with these words of the Canticle: "I to my Beloved and my Beloved to me." But these words were so transfigured for my soul that they seemed to be new. I felt my egoism and I understood how love is forgetful of self and I desired to concentrate my thoughts upon Jesus, as well as my affections, my works and my life. To live for him, to hand myself over to him totally. Finally, love and happiness are bound to that forgetfulness and to that surrender. The second part, entrancing and ineffable, is that Jesus is mine, totally mine.

Today, the third Sunday in Advent, a singular light upon what I preached in the cathedral, that is, that the habitual and constant attitude of the Christian ought to be joy. "Rejoice in the Lord always; again I say, rejoice, for the Lord is near."[2]

For the Christian the Lord is always near; in the Eucharist, in our heart, in our neighbor, in events of daily life. For us especially, the Lord is intimately near, ineffably near, in so many and in such endearing ways.

What can rob us of our joy? The solicitude of life? The Apostle forbids it: "In nothing be solicitous." That word of the Apostle has for me a special flavor. At first sight I ought to go around solicitous about many things; I have so many and such serious problems. But a comforting, astonishing experience has taught me that Jesus solves all my problems in an unforeseen way and with wonderful promptitude. May he guide me like a child, like a hypnotized person, that I may fulfill the marvel of the pact of San Antonio.

Those graces, although they were more intense each Sunday, extended their influence to the entire week; fortunately, my Advent has been one of light, consolation and love.

And assuming the charm that Christmas, my feast par excellence, always has for me, how shall I relish it now?

I think that in reality the love of God is not that of a spouse nor of a father nor a friend nor a son, but of God; that is, something unique that does not fit into any mold but which contains them all, heavenly manna having all savors, and which, therefore, is known to each soul as each soul needs it, according to its desires, its mission, its paths.

In these latter times (1940), paternal love has increased in me notably. Each day I feel myself more intensely a father and perhaps a grandfather, for such tenderness is more properly that of a grandfather. Hence, I conjecture what Jesus is going to make known to me next Christmas.

It must have been something very special, for he covered it with the veil of silence, leaving no memorandum about it. On February 14, 1941, the twenty-fifth anniversary of the grace of

---

[2] Mass of the third Sunday of Advent.

that date in 1916, he wrote:

Each day I feel more keenly the bliss of being insignificant; it is a happiness of an esthetic character, if I may be permitted that word. Surely our Lord has granted me a bit of the delight that his divine heart feels in the presence of littleness.

Be that as it may, it seems to me that I have found the formula to express the rapturous reality of the grace of February 14, 1916, when I say that Jesus is too great for one soul alone; therefore it was necessary that two souls unite to receive the unspeakable gift.

Together with gratitude, this grace demands that each day I make greater progress; since the best gratitude consists in using better the gifts bestowed.

I think that I have used it, during these twenty-five years, especially in dealing with souls; since, as Monsignor Gay asserts, one of the fruits of this kind of grace is to make the recipient soul more competent in dealing supernaturally with others.

But, how many deficiencies I find in my soul! How many shortcomings that contrast strikingly with the opulent graces that I have received from God.

To utilize better the precious grace, henceforth I desire: a new love for Jesus, a more generous surrender, a more ardent desire of giving him pleasure, of giving him glory.

When one feels God's grace, as I on this unforgettable evening am experiencing the grace of this anniversary, it seems to reach even the poor place of exile like a breeze from the Fatherland, like a gleam of eternal happiness. Blessed be the Lord who, not satisfied with making exile transitory and the Fatherland eternal, is pleased from time to time to sketch upon the cloud of this life some rays of celestial light.

On Christmas, 1941, he writes:

What better way to show the allurements of divine love (first mission) than to feel and express the mystery of Bethlehem? Mystery of smallness and of majesty! Mystery of love and of sacrifice!

Jesus is always divinely attractive; but the Child Jesus has an appealing aspect very suited to our littleness. Seeing him as a

Child, we feel him to be more like ourselves, and the likeness is a source of love. The gladness of Easter is deeper and more complete, more like the joy of heaven; it requires more depth in the soul's gaze, a love refined in sacrifice, a purification more intense and an elevation loftier so that our conversation may be in heaven, as St. Paul says. The happiness of Christmas is more ready, more human, an ingenuous joy, the joy of children. With what confidence we may approach the Child Jesus! One can always deal with children in untrammelled liberty.

For us Christmas has an unusual fascination, because in Bethlehem the mystery of weakness shines out singularly; we touch greatness, glory and love in God become a Child, inclosed in the fragile vase of smallness.

Although we are separated by a great distance, our souls, steeped in humility, confidence and love, will enjoy together on the most holy night, the divine mystery of Bethlehem.

May it be the celestial Babe's wish to make us more humble, more trustful, more childlike and to increase divine love in our souls.

On Christmas, 1942, he writes:

Christmas has for me a secret, exquisite delight, not only because on that day I sang my first Mass, now thirty-eight years ago, but especially because the mystery of Bethlehem suits admirably the engaging cast of my love.

The Child Jesus is my Jesus. Who can comprehend all the loveliness of that phrase? I surmise what St. Joseph must have felt on that most holy night in Bethlehem: a joy, a tenderness, a yearning for abnegation that we cannot begin to understand.

Each Christmas is with reason the sweetest one for me, whatever the state of my soul; on that night I always feel a consolation and a tenderness that make me shed unrestrained tears.

December 25. Last night, during the solemn Matins in the cathedral, when I heard the Invitatory: "Christ is born for us; come, let us adore," I was moved to tears. Those emotions cannot be described; but from the depths of the ineffable, considerations and resolutions can, indeed, be drawn forth.

Here is what I could realize: the joy of possessing Jesus; the certainty that he will purify my soul from many trifles that I had noticed lately, for holy Church in the Advent liturgy promises us that Jesus, born mystically in our hearts, relieves us of all our ills and transforms us spiritually; a new surrender of love; the promise to forget my own self.

December 29. Every time that I have preached during these days I have placed what I am going to say in the framework of Christmas, for this mystery possesses my soul. On one of those days I gave a Holy Hour entirely upon the Child Jesus: it came out well, but afterward they told me that my love for the Child Jesus was overflowing. This embarrassed me, because intimacies are only for friends; but, on the other hand, it gave me pleasure; for if love comes forth, it is a sign that love is there.

During this jubilant octave our Lord has cheered me up with consolation. Blessed may he be! Consolations are very useful for preserving peace in the midst of my many responsibilities.

We could continue observing how his love for the Child Jesus kept on increasing on successive Christmas Days. A lover of the splendor of the liturgy, he was accustomed to preside at Matins in the cathedral; to pontificate at midnight; after some few hours of sleep, to say the second Mass in his private oratory and, finally, to pontificate and preach at the day-time Mass. In the year 1954, he could no longer do so on account of his illness; but he celebrated the three Masses in his oratory.

He celebrated the Christmas Masses in his oratory in 1955 also, in silence, without any splendor; but, perhaps, on that last Christmas Eve, the Child Jesus made him an appointment for heaven, for that eternal Christmas which begins but never ends.

Another characteristic of Archbishop Martínez' love for Jesus was *confidence;* but confidence of a unique type. He trusted and he taught souls to trust, not only in spite of their own miseries, but precisely on account of them, since it is misery that attracts mercy. We have already had occasion to explain this doctrine; let us limit ourselves now to quoting some personal notes.

God is wonderful: upon the coarse cloth of our wretchedness he paints nothing less than the image of his Son, so much the more wonderful as the cloth is the more rough.

A few days ago, I was thinking about two attractions: the one which God exerts upon our souls and the one that we exert upon God; for if there is mutual love between God and the soul, there must be mutual attraction.

The first, how strong and how gentle! The whole history of souls is here: "I have loved thee with an everlasting love, therefore, full of mercy, I have drawn you." It is the eternal love, drenched with mercy, that attracts wretchedness. We feel the attraction of that infinite abyss of light and of love.

But God also feels the attraction of the abyss: the depth of our misery draws him. Thus, the mystery of our mutual love is accomplished. Is not the mercy of God something incomprehensible and yet most appealing?"

And in another place:

I saw mercy, gentle and caressing as the touch of a mother; ardent as a kiss, enraptured with love; immense as an ocean. It is the love that pardons, heals, cherishes, elevates and promises union.

Sometimes I am overwhelmed with its greatness, but a greatness tempered by love; sometimes it seemed to me that love—because mercy is love disguised by a divine veil—descended even to the depths of my nothingness, and possessed it, healing what was infirm, cleansing what was stained, elevating what was low.

Yes, mercy is love assuming that gracious name to descend even to the miserable, even to sinners. One would say that it is love made expressly for me. Love with a tone of delicacy, of tenderness, of boldness, of kindness; love with a transforming power, capable of changing nothingness into something divine, love for whose enticement there is no apology, for whose effusions there is no embarrassment; it seems so natural for mercy to love misery!

And that mercy is infinite. Under its action, the soul feels not only the consolation of pardon, but the holy security of love, as the pledge of union.

Mercy is love that makes stained souls virginal, that cleanses, pardons and forgets so divinely that the soul, without failing to perceive its wretchedness, but rather, feeling it as never before, aspires without boldness to what only virginal souls have a right to aspire.

It seemed to me that mercy was speaking to me saying: "I have become intensely enamored of your misery, therefore, full of compassion for you, I have attracted you."

To be loved in this way is to be loved very delicately, divinely.

Can there be more convincing pages to incite confidence despite misgivings? Very appropriately he concludes: "I continue receiving from God lights and special graces which indicate to me how much he loves me."

Our Lord taught His Excellency the doctrine of the "mystery of weakness" and it so penetrated his soul that he made it the program of his life and he incorporated it into his episcopal coat of arms, as we have seen. Each day God made him know better the profoundity and the importance of that mystery.

I think that all our aberrations and failings come from the fact that we do not have deep knowledge of ourselves and of God. Our misery is so deep that it seems we never reach the bottom; and because we never finish getting acquainted with it, we are frightened by our imperfections.

And especially, God is so great in all his attributes that not even in eternity shall we come to full understanding of him. If we knew his beauty, how we would love him! If we realized his power and his kindness, how we would trust in him and abandon ourselves to him! If we understood how much he loves us, how we would adore his will! If we knew his mercy, what assurance of his pardon and his love!

The "mystery of weakness" acquaints us with our *nothingness* and God's *Allness,* and expresses the relations existing between these two extremes. Happy the soul that has understood the intense fascination of those relations, the soul that has known through its own experience what it is to have nothingness supported by All-ness and, on that account, has understood the value and the charm of miseries and has been pleased with them.

But not all souls, or to speak more accurately, very few souls, comprehend this mystery.

I have observed that almost all the obstacles which souls find on the path to perfection can be reduced to this: they do not know how to behave well in respect to their imperfections; they do not know how to make them a ladder to go to God. And in the final analysis, the reason is that they understand neither their own limitations nor the infinite mercy of God.

Ordinarily souls are held back by temptations, defects and desolations, that is to say, miseries. Souls judge these to be obstacles to going to God but in reality they are stairs leading directly to him.

Evidently souls are disconcerted by these miseries because they have the appearance of something that alienates us from God. It is so difficult at times to discriminate between temptation and sin. Few persons distinguish between the offense given to God by a fault and the resultant ignominy for the soul, which, properly understood, brings us a deeper knowledge of ourselves. How natural it is to see in desolations an abandonment, a separation from God!

I believe that the secret for travelling speedily on the path of perfection is to change those obstacles into stairs; but to do that, one must have a clear view of those miseries and a profound knowledge of the mercy, kindness and *mode of being* of God. In a word, one needs a deep penetration of the "mystery of weakness."

There are souls who attain that penetration in ordinary obstacles, but who waver in the presence of extraordinary onslaughts, such as strange, violent, terrible temptations, but simply temptations, since the will remains intimately united to God.

Elsewhere, we have called these "temptations of the mystical life." The will would prefer death to offending God. A comparison clarifies this matter.

On the high sea, a fine line seems to separate the sky from the ocean; and, nevertheless, an immense distance exists between the two. So it happens with temptations; they seem to be mixed up with sin and, nevertheless, there is between the two the immense distance that separates hate from love.

Someone may object: "Although temptations may not be sin, do they not have a close relationship with sin that makes them abominable?"

Jesus, sanctity itself, desired to be tempted, and with his temptations he gave immense glory to the heavenly Father and with his triumph he obtained victory for us, also.

There is an immense difference, no doubt, between Jesus' temptations and ours; because in him there could be no inclination toward the object of the temptation, as there is in our case. But this only indicates our misery and nothing but our misery, because those inclinations are from the lower appetite, not from the will. The will is the only faculty that consummates sin when there is sin, and the only faculty that loves God. Consequently, it is the will that consummates our union with God on this earth.

What a beautiful spectacle the will presents, strongly united to God, while below, in the inferior part of the soul the tempest is raging! It is a martyrdom comparable to those in which the serenity of the martyrs prevailed in the midst of the fury of the wild beasts in the Roman amphitheater. What does it matter that the martyr's flesh often trembles in face of torment and the lower faculties become horror-stricken, if the will, united to God and strengthened by him, offers and completes the holocaust?

What must Jesus think when he sees souls in those terrible combats? He thinks just what he must have thought when he saw the martyrs for the faith. He looks upon them with tenderness, with satisfaction, with immense complacency. How could his heart help but be pleased with the martyrdom of virginity? "Have you seen my servant Job," said God. "You have wounded him and he thanks me; you have ruined him and he does not blaspheme; you have killed his children and he blesses me."

How deep God's complacency when he sees his poor creature

cast about by trial and who, nevertheless, clings to him in love. He must say to the angels: "Have you seen my beloved, how faithful, how steadfastly united to me in the midst of torments and tempests?"

Those tempted souls must believe this: in those frightful moments they give glory to God, they strengthen virtue, they obtain graces for other souls. This being true, why not even be pleased with those miseries, since they form a part of the mystery of weakness? When God desires a soul to attain a virtue, he often permits it to be tempted against that virtue; when he desires it to achieve that virtue to an extraordinary degree, the temptations are also extraordinary. God always does things the reverse of our poor judgment. *Cum infirmor, tunc potens sum,* will always be true.

Probably some one will complain to me: "What was it for God to send me another trial, a sickness, for example, or a humiliation?"

God is the great artist of souls: He strikes them to beautify them, to make them what he has envisoned. Does it seem of small moment that an artist sacrifices his ideal? Without the trial it would cost God that exquisite pleasure he experiences upon seeing a soul come out of the mud hole cleaner, with its love finer and more ardent after the trial.

Why are souls so unacquainted with Jesus? Do they not know that he will never permit them to be separated from him? Then let them trust him fully; let them cast themselves into his arms with their eyes closed, for in this case, too, love must be blind. He sees, he understands. Above all, must not the soul give him pleasure? Let her give him that intimate pleasure although she may be suffering the sorrows of hell. How sweet, how glorious, to give pleasure, especially interiorly, at the cost of our own broken heart!

In another place he writes:

Many a time my soul needs heroic confidence. The obstacle to its possession comes from looking too much at ourselves and not knowing how to look at God; from a double ignorance: of God and of ourselves. Our imperfections attract our attention, as an acorn-bearing oak would attract the attention of one not knowing that tree. And not knowing to what lengths infinite love and mercy extend, it costs effort to trust fully in God and to assume before him the attitude of greater confidence and intimacy when the acorns of our frailty appear.

For one who knows or has an intimation of what the heart of God is, heroic confidence is the most natural thing in the world. But, how difficult it is to become acquainted with that heart without wanting to put it into the narrow mold of our own! I think that one of the supreme revelations of the divine heart is that which engenders this heroic confidence.

The Archbishop certainly received that revelation since he eventually acquired heroic confidence.

Only an infinite heart, a measureless love, can love us in spite of everything, and even increase the tenderness when we are overwhelmed by our own wretchedness. How great, how beautiful, how sweet the heart of Jesus appears when we know it in such a way! It would be enough to make us fall in love with him, to love him with perfect love!

He reveals to us the secret of eventually obtaining this revelation.

But for this revelation, it is necessary to stop looking at ourselves and to leave off looking at Jesus through our own smallness. Heroic confidence is a beautiful homage paid to mercy and to the Beloved.

The only thing which attracts that love plentifully is the emptiness of our own wretchedness; he persists in deepening it more and more so that more and more of his loving, divine plenitude may fit within.

In the many cases in which I have prescribed that marvelous remedy for souls, I have seen its happy results; but it always seems a novelty to these persons. A novelty that has been upon the earth for twenty centuries!

I apply this heroic confidence to the situation in Mexico, to the government of this archdiocese and even to the most prosaic problems of life. For all cases the supreme remedy is to leave off looking at ourselves and to look at him, but to look at him in the splendor of his loving mercy.

I had always believed that my specialty was confidence and I even applied to myself the expression in the Psalms: "Thou hast singularly established me in hope." But very recently I have seen that something was lacking to me; the summits of virtue are so lofty that a great deal is missing through our frailty.

With the sincere ingenuity of one who gives testimony of himself in the presence of God, Archbishop Martínez writes:

A short time ago our Lord made me see, with that clarity characteristic of his communications, that my limitations are not an obstacle to his love for my soul and that I am very pleasing to him. Rather, in the hands of his mercy, those imperfections either are instruments of sanctification or are converted into them.

First, he made me perceive what he does through me: the remarkable efficacy which he communicates to my words and to my heart; for I cannot doubt that he, through me, leads souls to sanctity.

Then it dawned on me that in the eyes of God my soul is purer and holier than I thought it was.

A few days ago during Holy Mass, he caused me to see still more clearly that my soul is pleasing in his eyes. On Holy Thursday night I felt a most vivid invitation to open my heart and discuss with him this most important matter (of miseries) in utmost sincerity. He communicated himself to me in light and in joy, and I saw clearly, although my reason does not fully explain it, that he loves me and what he has given me, and I saw my soul pure and pleasing to him; and the barrier was broken and our intimacy became utterly delightful.

Only the humblest of souls could speak in this way. Such was Archbishop Martínez. But let us see to what a point his confidence reached.

Some days ago I had a special light for understanding intimacy with God and I felt its attraction keenly. In my judgment, intimacy consists in the mutual right of the lovers to enter each other's heart at any time, even to the innermost recesses and without knocking; just as one would in his own house.

As both hearts are one single heart, the one is always at the disposition of the other. Whenever we wish we can enter that infinite heart and take refuge there, and we can rest and feel that exquisite, delightful satisfaction of another heart being our own and we can enjoy its loving treasures.

Where there is intimacy, there are no secrets; my heart is open to the gaze of the Beloved even to its farthest corners. I can enter even to the depths of the divine heart that holds no secrets from me except those imposed by his infinity and my limitations. I can enter that heart as my own house, whenever it pleases me, without knocking.

The life of two in one single, solitary thing has unspeakable delights: the joy of love, the peace of unity and the fullness of rest. With that intimacy, one can endure the burden of human life, which is very heavy for one soul alone, because the pressure of suffering like the pressure of happiness is so great that it can only be supported by two. That intimacy lightens even the yoke of the priestly life, which abounds more in both sorrows and joys than all other ways of life.

I cannot explain all I saw and felt, but he who has experienced it will understand me.

Then he immediately speaks of his saint's day, which he was accustomed to observe each year in one form or other:

On my saint's day, our Lord gave me a present, the best present: from the night of the twentieth he united himself with me most ardently, showering me with caresses. All next day was perfumed with love and I spent it more content than ever before. On the night of the twenty-first, a new disclosure of love, something very deep and inexplicable.

He was my gift; but what moved me most was not so much the gift as the love with which he gave it to me. He made me understand—it embarrasses me even to write it!—that he was satisfied to be mine. Naturally, in the midst of the transports of my happiness,

I surrendered myself to him without reserve and I felt the immense happiness of being his.

I had another intuition, also: with a new light I saw the unity and the simplicity of love, and how any affection that is not established upon divine love is opposed to them. In other terms, I felt a kind of horror lest anyone love me, if not in him and lest I love anyone outside of him. Never as now had I comprehended the meaning of purity and virginity of heart.

One night a very sweet, intimate union took place. Previously, I began to feel God's call, for now I know when he wants to speak to me or to do something in my soul. I made him wait until I finished the Office and all the rest of my customary prayers.

In the midst of the union he made me understand that he wants a more complete intimacy with me, but he made no explanation. The person who said that a grace has three elements was right: the grace itself, our recognition of the grace, and the deep import of the grace.

Little by little, the *new* intimacy is becoming clearer to me, but I still cannot explain it adequately. He wants to live fully in me and I must lose myself entirely in him. How? I still do not know it all. I only know that he, in me, desires to do all my work, suggest everything to me, actuate me in everything, and that I respond to him. I must enter far within his heart, in the boundless refuge of his love.

The genuinely mystical character of these graces is self-evident. But many souls would arrive at this stupendous familiarity if they would learn to trust, if they were not stultified in their wretchedness, if notwithstanding they would cast their miseries into the depths of infinite mercy.

Some days later our Lord resumed explaining to him this *new* familiarity.

Our Lord has kept explaining it to me, usually during the night when we can discuss the matter with greater liberty, but also at times during the day when I can visit him and in all places, especially on the train, when I succeed in being alone, which is seldom.

His explanation can be expressed in this formula: *To allow myself to be possessed and guided by him in everything and to lose myself in him.*

The first part of that formula signifies that I may do nothing without having recourse to him, that I consult him, that I let him guide me, that I do only what pleases him, that I live only to give him pleasure. Basically, it is the same thing he once sent me word to do—rest in his love, trust him without measure, allow him to guide me and depend totally upon him.

The second part signifies that I enter his love, his heart, the ocean of his goodness; but with such a forgetfulness of myself that I lose myself in him.

Some examples explain this: when we hear a musical composition or contemplate a beautiful spectacle, sometimes, in the midst of the delightful impressions we experience, the consciousness of ourselves and of what we are enjoying remains; but when we hear or contemplate something sublime, consciousness of ourselves is completely lost and the subjective reaction is no longer perceived; we are caught up by the beauty of what we are enjoying; we are lost then in that captivating impression.

To be lost in God is something similar: to be captivated in such a way by his beauty, his immensity, that we forget ourselves so that he and his perfections may fill and absorb us.

We can lose ourselves in him, not only in contemplation but also in love. Sometimes we love him by preserving, so to speak, the notion of ourselves and by feeling our relations with him; but sometimes love possesses our heart in such a way that he, the most absorbing object of our love, makes us forget ourselves completely and withdraw from ourselves, as it were. As St. Denis said: "Love produces ecstasy," for the essence of ecstasy is not precisely in the suspension of the senses, but in that blessed departure from our own selves.

The intimacy is akin to the essence of spiritual childhood.

Jesus desires my soul to be familiar with him as a child. In the case of a child, trust is unlimited, contact is simple and daring.

What hinders us from embracing a child, pressing him against our heart, kissing him as we please, permitting ourselves all the liberties of tenderness?

Jesus desires me to deal with him in this way, as if he were a child, although I may consider him in any of the mysteries of his life. Association in this way brings us an absolute and very close familiarity. We thereby place ourselves in contact with the divine, the only thing that fills the soul, satisfies love and satiates our deep aspirations.

Child, to attract me to intimacy; God, to satiate me with the divine, with the light, the beauty, the happiness of the divinity. It is evident that for such intimacy I need purity and candor, simplicity and audacity, all the qualities of spiritual childhood. Shall I reach that perfect intimacy?

Archbishop Martínez certainly did reach it. He wrote the foregoing notes twenty-four years before his death and as each day he advanced higher in holy intimacy, at the end of his life he arrived at the summit.

We could point out other characteristics of Archbishop Martínez' love; for example, he loved Jesus *humbly*. When he approached the tabernacle, he could do nothing but love and abase himself, that is to say, *adore*. Is not adoration a marvelous combination of self-abasing love and of loving self-abasement?

But the humility of the Archbishop, like that of the saints, was baffling. When he speaks of his miseries—and he speaks so much of them—we want to give them the realistic meaning which they have in the case of simple mortals like ourselves, whereas they are only the expression of a humility whose depth makes us suspect the height of sanctity to which God elevated him; the clarity with which he contemplated the allness of God, which by contrast made him feel his own nothingness.

As Jesus' love increased before my eyes, mine diminished and became repugnant. Is it really love that I bear in my heart so full of egoism, so paltry, so limited, so faulty? How Jesus' total surrender to me contrasts with my consecration to him—if it may be so called—which does not hinder me from seeking myself and arguing with Jesus over the demands of love! I can scarcely say that I love! I must exert myself to love in reality.

In another place he says:

Sometimes I see nothing in my soul but soiled, coarse rags; and I have come to fear that is all there is in it. But Jesus takes care to show himself to me from time to time across the rags. I could call that manifestation, the epiphany of the rags. Through them, I discover in those fleeting moments, the obverse: *love, union.*

I carry celestial treasures in a fragile vessel. Alas, too fragile! Too unlovely! My motto is most appropriate: *Cum infirmor, tunc potens sum.*

Of late, there have dominated in my soul the clear thought and the deep feeling that I am nothing, I can do nothing, I have nothing. Jesus is my treasure, my power, my life, my all. What secret happiness the soul enjoys upon feeling her nothingness, knowing that God is her All and relishing this truth!

Who would have thought that it could be so satisfying to have nothing, to be able to do nothing, to be nothing? It is not simply the happiness of being exceedingly rich with our All, but especially the happiness of owing it all to love, of depending upon the Beloved in everything and for everything.

Sometimes I play the noble, preferring to love rather than to be loved; but one night, near the tabernacle I felt the necessity of being loved and of artlessly seeking Jesus' love.

Little by little my knowledge of that need of my soul deepened and I felt poor, stripped, nothing; but I saw how he is my wealth and my all. Since then I enjoy that double happiness, being nothing and having everything.

The Archbishop taught that union of the soul with God is accomplished when both profundities are united. The Word descends from heaven and, becoming man, plunges himself into an abyss of abasement. The soul, through perfect humility, plunges herself also into the abyss of her own nothingness. And in the bottom of two chasms, the Word and the soul meet and are united.

If Archbishop Martínez loved Jesus so much, where would he seek him but in the Eucharist, where he is found in a manner so real, so concrete, so intimate, so favorable to the outpourings of love. Therefore his love had a profoundly *Eucharistic* tone.

After he became titular Bishop, he obtained an indult from the Holy See to keep the Blessed Sacrament in his private oratory. This took place in October, 1924. From then until his death, he passed the most delightful hours of his life before his tabernacle; there he went to rest from his apostolic fatigues and to receive light for himself and for souls. There, especially, how much love and consolation our Lord received, as he himself deigned to manifest to him!

Whenever His Excellency left the house or returned to it, he made a brief visit to his chapel; whenever he had a moment during the day, he hastened to spend it at the foot of the altar. But, especially, between half past ten and eleven o'clock at night, when the rigorous labor of the day was ended, and all had retired and the house was wrapped in silence in the shades of night, he went to his oratory and there spent "delightful hours," as he said, and at times he literally had to do himself violence to tear himself away from his tabernacle for rest when the night was already far advanced.

But it was during his spiritual exercises, made with utmost fidelity each year, that he indulged in the pleasure of extending those "delightful hours." I myself could verify that during the retreat he had only two apportionments of time daily; but one filled the whole morning and the other, the entire afternoon.

And with what devoted delicacy and liturgical taste he arranged his oratory, especially the last! There was nothing in it but the altar and tabernacle, artistically carved in fine wood, a large crucifix under a baldachino, four candlesticks and the curtains surrounding the altar. A beautiful restraint in contrast to so many oratories that, however small, look as if almost the whole heavenly court wish to enter there!

In Jerez I had a special light: we do not begin to comprehend to what a point Jesus is *ours* in Holy Communion. Afterwards I had another union: I understood in a way that touched my heart how one Mass consoles and satisfies Jesus, the satisfaction and comfort that we give him by lending our assistance to that sublime, transcendent act. Only God knows what it costs me to fail to celebrate one Mass. Well then, it costs Jesus more, speaking in our language.

Therefore, on his trips he did even the impossible in order to celebrate Mass. For example, on a trip to Europe he postponed his breakfast until two o'clock in the afternoon, expecting to land on the Azores and offer Mass there. But the plane was behind schedule and he lost all hope.

On those occasions when he was obliged to forego the offering of Mass, he used to say a "spiritual Mass," the conception of Bishop Leopoldo Ruiz, which he taught to Archbishop Martínez. It consists in reading over all the parts of the Mass, entering into the spirit of each one of them. Externally, nevertheless, he made no ostentation; when it was necessary, he gave up celebrating with all naturalness and no one suspected the sacrifice entailed.

In the last two years, the celebration of Mass cost him a great sacrifice for he had lost the use of his right eye through arteriosclerosis, while he could see with great difficulty with his left eye and only with a large lens. He did not want, nevertheless, to ask for the indult which the Holy See grants to priests who have partially lost their sight. In the final days of his illness he sometimes had to delay the holy Mass until midday.

In another place he writes:

Our Lord wants me in peace, consoled, secure. One morning the devil tried to upset me, but simply at the sight of the tabernacle, my heart was filled with joy and security in the love of Jesus. What did he do to dispel the clouds from my soul in one instant?

Jesus is impelling and enkindling me, sometimes as if he made the veils covering his beauty transparent in order to inflame me. Last night in the parish church I was carrying out the ritual for the opening of the visitation. When speaking to the people I felt very recollected; all was in peace. But when I opened the tabernacle, when my hands touched the sacred vessel, and particularly when I took off the veil covering it, the sacred host revealed itself to me, I know not what I felt, as if he himself had revealed himself to me. I could not see that host. . . .

After the Blessed Sacrament was exposed, they prayed the Rosary and I remained on the priedieu, struggling between seeing and not seeing the host. I yearned to see it yet I wanted to close my eyes. Is it not true that there are times when the soul cannot "bear" Jesus? Can it be modesty, fear of happiness, love's martyrdom? Who can explain it? A very delightful sorrow and a very sorrowful delight.

Holy Thursday was heaven for me. Fortunately they left me in peace; and after the Office, I spent an hour before the Most Holy impregnating myself, as it were, with the interior sentiments of the Sacred Heart on that unforgettable night.

Afterwards I read very attentively the sermon at the Last Supper and I saw the love of Jesus *in a new way,* surprising me as if then I had the first revelation of that love. That love is always new, although it has at the same time the exquisite savor of the old, of what is familiar to us, of what is imbued with the perfume of our personal remembrance.

The tenderness of Jesus with St. John especially attracted my attention. To allow him to recline on his bosom! To allow him to rest on his heart! To answer the disciple when he asked about the traitor! Jesus would have that tenderness with all souls if they would offer themselves, if they should like it, if they had the love and the daring of the beloved disciple.

Apropos of the procession in which he carried the sacred host so near, he asked himself how he could withstand that proximity, in the light of the knowledge and the love of Jesus granted to him.

I think that sometimes the cause is imperfections and infidelity; sometimes, a divine dispensation. But in me there are two beings, as it were: one spiritual and the other human, and they help each other.

One day, disturbed by certain difficulties, I approached the tabernacle and he so showed me his complacency and love that I felt happy. His divine kiss filled me with peace.

Archbishop Martínez could not live without his tabernacle. On one occasion his house was confiscated and he had to leave the city. Upon returning, he found himself without the Blessed Sacrament. The following day he again placed the Sacred Host there. "But I noticed," he says, "in those houses, that I cannot live without Jesus, without him whom I bear within me, without him who is in the tabernacle. During this period he has been exceedingly good to me. How much sweetness he pours into my heart in our nightly intimacies!"

On another occasion a very troubled person approached His Excellency and to console the sufferer he said understandingly:

"You cannot be sad on a day on which you have received Communion. One Communion is enough to fill a day with joy."

And I realized that I live with Jesus, with the Jesus of my interior life and with the Jesus of my tabernacle, as St. Joseph lived with Jesus in Nazareth. If I descend to the profundity of the supernatural, my life is Nazareth, it is heaven. Jesus is the sun of my life. He solves all my problems for me, he encourages me, he fills me with joy and with peace.

Of late I have done two things instinctively when I approach the tabernacle: I abase myself and I tell him untiringly that I love him. I could not live alone: what would I do without him? Lately, especially, I have the impression that I am living with him, *in his household*. He is the treasure of my life and the Master of my heart.

I need his inspiration, his action, his help; but more, much more,

I need his love. I understand that I correspond very poorly to his love; but what is delightful about our union is the fact that he puts up with me. So I need a *forbearing Lover*. Wrapped in my miseries, I belong to him.

To unite himself to us in an ineffable manner and to give himself to us without measure and to immolate himself at each instant for our love, he instituted the Eucharist through which he becomes our companion, our life and our ransom.

To return him love for love and gift for gift, we have to make our own eucharist, poor and limited like ourselves, but at least our own gift. To live in union with him, to give ourselves to him without measure, to immolate ourselves for his love—this is to convert ourselves into a *living eucharist*. Jesus' Eucharist was the fruit of an infinite love and of an ineffable sacrifice, in the Cenacle and on the Cross; for us, love and sacrifice will produce our eucharist.

But perhaps the elements of the Eucharist are not sufficiently enumerated. That love and that sacrifice of Jesus presuppose divine purity. He loved us so, he gave himself to us in such a way, he immolated himself for us as he did, through the divine unity of his purity.

To make our eucharist, we need first to attain a great perfection of purity, detaching ourselves from everything; forgetting our own selves, so that, in the unity of that purity, we may be able to have the love and the fructifying suffering that produce our eucharist. Magnificent spiritual program!

The past week I gave the retreat to thirty-five priests; it seems to have been a success. One afternoon I spoke to them of the love of Jesus, which is the key of the priestly life, and especially of love for the Holy Eucharist and of the care we ought to have for all that appertains to it. Who would have thought that on that night Jesus would show his gratitude, uniting himself to my soul in a special manner and showing me his love as he knows how to do? How grateful Jesus is! How refined! "Just as the holy Virgin trained him," said Señora Armida very felicitously.

Another characteristic of Archbishop Martínez' love was

his passion for fulfilling the will of God; and his entire will, not only his signified will but that of simple good pleasure. "To give pleasure to the Beloved," as he used to say.

Jesus has imparted to me a placid confidence in his love, and he has poured into me the interior joy of doing his will, whatever it may be. I am disposed for all that he may wish; even more, I feel joyous that what he wishes is done.

And in these three impressions he discovers the mystery of love: "the Beloved possessed, the Beloved doing my work and my will, I doing the work and the will of the Beloved."

Later he writes: "Since to love is to give pleasure to the Beloved, I want always to do what pleases him. Love transforms all life's bitterness into sweetness, since the one who loves sees in everything the will, the pleasure of the Beloved."

And in another place:

The joys of love are the contemplation of the Beloved, his possession and the fulfillment of his will.

We cannot prevent earthly things from impressing us; but we must divinize these impressions, so to speak, converting them into love.

This two-fold consideration which is intertwined with the preceding has served greatly to maintain peace in my soul. I wish to do the will of the Beloved in everything and he also wishes to give me pleasure in everything that is in harmony with his will. Consequently, I ought to take joy in everything that happens to me, because the will of the Beloved disposes or permits it all. No difficulty, no problem should preoccupy me, because he does everything for me, arranges everything for me, because in everything which is becoming he wishes to give me pleasure. Thus my soul is in peace, a peace which is a copy of heaven.

On another occasion he writes:

I have had a season of lights and consolations. Three things especially Jesus has made me desire and he has granted them: the desire of being always with him in the midst of occupations and vicissitudes. He has given me a great security that he is with me and a conviction that he is the only one who does not change, who does not abandon, who puts up with everything in us, a conviction that with him I am never alone, that I always depend on him.

The second is a confidence, an abandonment to his love which takes away all anxiety because it gives me the assurance that he is arranging everything, however difficult it may seem to me. This is a source of peace and well-being.

The third is the desire of giving him pleasure in everything, even at the cost of sacrifices, because love demands it and because to give him pleasure is a deep joy....

There persists in my soul the resolution and the desire of giving him pleasure in all things, even in the most harrowing affairs, with the help of his grace. Does not love consist in satisfying the Beloved?

Another thing that I have experienced is the desire and the joy of giving pleasure to Jesus. Even what is painful seems pleasant to me when I realize that I am doing his will, that I am giving him pleasure.

When we perceive what it is that is loved, we yearn for the full possession of heaven and for that possession of the land which, according to St. John of the Cross, "knows eternal life."

The soul also feels the imperious necessity of giving itself, of seeking, of doing the will of the Beloved and of taking satisfaction in it. To possess him and to give oneself to him! The substance of love!

Quotations such as these could be multiplied. The *total surrender* is an act that he repeats innumerable times; and each one marks a new ascent in his spiritual life. And what does "total surrender" mean but the full adhesion to God's will?

This passion for the divine will was particularly prominent in his last years. Then, especially, could be applied to his soul those beautiful words of one whom he directed: "My soul is rowing on the high sea where there are seen only the immense heaven of the will of God and the fathomless sea of my confidence in him."

If it were not for fear of being endless, we would continue describing other aspects of Archbishop Martínez' love, but since we must close this matter, we shall limit ourselves to pointing out in conclusion one final tone of his love.

His love was specifically divine.

My life this month was very agitated on account of the enormous work of the visitation. But in the midst of business I had many communications with Jesus, for I spent almost the entire day in the church administering confirmation to more than seven thousand, and hearing confessions.

Jesus made me understand that he wants to raise me to another spiritual stage, with a more interior knowledge of him, with a deeper love, with a closer union.

The indispensable condition for this is perfect virginity of heart which comprises two parts: neither to love nor to allow myself to be loved by any creature, neither to wish to please anyone nor to please myself. This is perfect purity, free from all affection, especially from self-love. And he made me see many deficiencies in these points.

With this virginity of heart, charity will be fully developed and it will be poured out abundantly in souls. Moreover, Jesus assures me that this plenitude of charity will come through the paths which I have just pointed out.

On many occasions he has made me notice what I ought to avoid and he has even cared for me singularly; but the devil, too, has prepared for me special struggles.

He adds another very beautiful sentence which completes the preceding lessons:

I understood how the most precious thing is to love the divine. The Word of God, who from all eternity has loved us divinely, upon coming to earth "learned" to love us humanly by an exquisite, ineffable delicacy. And he taught us to love divinely. To love in this way is not only to love with perfect purity, with in-

credible profundity, with exquisite tenderness; but it is in truth
to love as God loves, that is to say, to love as the Father loves the
Son, and as the Son loves the Father, that is, I say again, to love
through the Holy Spirit.

Charity, image of the Holy Spirit, makes us love in a divine
way; but to love in a true and perfect manner is to love under the
impulse of the Holy Spirit. One of the tones of that love is the
one that God has given me, because it is a reflection of the love
of the Father.

Further on, he says:

There is something of the incomplete and imperfect in my life;
my soul needs to surrender itself without reserve to love. I thirst
for contemplation and it seems to me that I allow myself to be
absorbed by occupations—although they may be holy—and I lose
those intimate communications with God that are heaven in
anticipation.

I spent an hour with the gaze of my soul fixed upon Jesus, great,
beautiful, loving, captivating my soul with his divine charms. Why
do I not look at him more, always?

He invited me as formerly to a more intimate knowledge of
him, to delve into the mystery of Christ, just as he proposed it to
me in the last retreat. For this I need a full, virginal, divine
love. Who will comprehend what each one of these words signifies? The heart free from earth, the soul forgotten by its very self
and that brand of love filling my life!

Upon reading that sentence of St. Paul: "We have received the
Spirit of adoption whereby we cry, Abba, Father!" I thought that
that same Spirit, since he is the love of the Father and of the
Son, also cries out in our souls: "Son! Son!" Never had I understood as now the doctrine of St. Thomas, that the apostolic life is
the overflowing of the contemplative life. I used to think that the
Angelic Doctor meant that the source of light, love and sacrifice
lies in contemplation, which waters the arid plains of action; that
all the efficacy of action comes from contemplation. I thought that
on the summit of loving light the mainspring is forged to carry
us to souls as well as the self-forgetting heroism that makes us

spend ourselves for them; that the heaven of contemplation diffuses upon the prosaic earth of action the immaterial beauty which idealizes and ennobles it.

But now I see something more profound: the distinction between contemplation and action in the apostolic life has something of the artificial; at least it is a fragmentation that the limitations of our spirit make in the rich, majestic unity of the spiritual life. To do good to souls it is not necessary to leave contemplation and to depart from intimacy with Jesus; rather, one must enter that divine region; it is like a copy of God's action upon creatures which does not make him come out of himself. If God were to have something to do in order to work outside of himself, it would be to concentrate himself in the profundities of his being; but he does not need to concentrate himself because he always lives in his infinite simplicity.

It is not necessary to leave the intimacy of Jesus to work in souls, if we understand that the entire Jesus, so to speak, embraces all souls. It is a form of intimacy with Jesus to preach, to direct, to govern, if all this is done in accordance with the supernatural, the divine.

If an apostolic soul absorbed in God had to do something in order to do good to souls, it would be only to plunge itself more deeply into the ocean of the divinity. To do an apostolic work is not to leave but to enter that august sanctuary. To do an apostolic work is to be filled with God to such a degree, that God, overflowing—to speak in our poor language—reaches souls and bathes them and penetrates them and gives them life.

CHAPTER VIII

Living Portrait of Christ

THE SECOND MISSION of Archbishop Martínez was to reproduce Christ, to be his living portrait. This signifies three things: to copy the virtues of Christ, to reproduce his mysteries mystically, and to do or to continue his work. In this way the desire of St. Paul is realized, to have the same sentiments as Christ—"Have in you this mind which is in Christ"—and to continue his work in such a way that the man disappears and only Christ remains to pursue in the world his work of salvation and redemption—"I live, but not I: Christ lives in me." These three aspects are so related and complementary that we cannot treat of one without treating of the others. Nevertheless, let us say something of each one.

Christ appeared in the world, *poor*. We can apply to Archbishop Martínez the words associated with St. Pius X: "He was born poor, he lived poor, and he died poor." His poverty was neither imposed nor compulsory, but entirely voluntary. He never lacked what was necessary and fitting according to his social position and ecclesiastical dignity. But he always gave away whatever he had and frequently even more than he had, trustful in divine providence that never failed him. He once said: "We bishops must sanctify ourselves in very special circumstances: we must be poor in abundance, mortified in spite of feasts and banquets, humble in the midst of honors."

Millions passed through his hands, but they did nothing more than pass. He gave it all to the poor, whom he called his episcopal family, and to the mighty works that he accomplished.

189

We have already seen how from the time of his episcopal consecration he gave to the poor all the confirmation stipends he received; therefore, when infirm, almost incapacitated, he continued administering this sacrament up to the end.

But that money was not sufficient. Many a time at the middle of the month his monthly allowance as Archbishop of Mexico City was already exhausted. His household knew of the difficulties and the penury in the daily expense of the house.

Like every intellectual man, he had a passion for books. On one occasion someone lent him a book by the well-known French critic, Jules Lemaître. This author pleased him so much that he commissioned me to buy certain other books by the same author. But soon he wrote to say that, if I had not yet sent the order, he would cancel it, because it seemed to him that this expense was not necessary, and there were so many needs!

His library was formed for the greater part by books given him as gifts. They were few, but very select, because his friends understood his tastes. The furniture of his house had also been given as gifts. In the same category were his pectoral crosses and crosiers; he never purchased a single one, until he became Archbishop of Mexico City, using only a simple pectoral cross without any ornament.

The writer arranged his baggage many times for his frequent trips; his personal effects were like those of any simple seminarian. Outside of Mexico City, he wore the episcopal hat; almost until his death, he used a very old and worn one which had belonged to Archbishop Arciga, second Archbishop of Michoacán, who had discarded it as unserviceable. A new one was purchased for Archbishop Martínez, without consulting him, in 1951, but he used it only a few times. In his diary, he writes ingenuously:

I give away all the money that falls to me; some think I carry it to excess, and sometimes I think so, too. But in spite of everything,

I have some savings which I have not spent, *because I don't have them here.* A few days ago I thought, through something they said to me, that I had lost them. And it pleased me that I stayed as unconcerned as if I had lost a button off my cassock, although it was a relatively considerable sum. Afterwards it became clear that nothing had been lost; but this affair helped me to sound my heart.[1]

It is costing me greater effort to keep my heart free from affections, because with the years I have become not only a father but a grandfather, spiritually. Of course, no heart is so rich in affection as that of the priest, but it is necessary to watch lest there be anything human in those affections, because for us Jesus is all and he is the only one.

Jesus was *meek* and *humble* of heart. As we have already seen, Archbishop Martínez' humility is disconcerting to one who does not know him thoroughly. Either he seems to exaggerate, and thus be insincere, or when he speaks so much about his "miseries" he may seem to discuss something blameworthy. In reality it was the great light given him to see, as he said, the allness of God and his own nothingness.

His humility was not exactly the so-called "humility of abjection" which brings us from self-knowledge to self-hatred. It was not a humility that makes us forget ourselves, disappear and die to ourselves. It was the humility of *smallness* of spiritual infancy.

From his first retreat until the last, there is always a resolution about humility. "It is my little hobby," he used to say. His humility was for him, above all, the great means to attain perfect love of God; he considered it as the death of egoism, of self-love, which is the great enemy of charity. He always saw humility in terms of love. For example, in the retreat of 1933, he writes: To reach a closer intimacy with Jesus, as he

[1] That is to say, to test his detachment.

is asking me and as I desire, I shall attempt two things: to disappear and to fill myself with him." Afterwards he enters into details for attaining the one and the other.

In the retreat of 1938 he writes: "Exquisite care to preserve myself in humility."

In the retreat of 1940 he records:

If love must be the foundation of my life, I should analyze the characteristics of this love. Above all, it must fill my heart completely: I must love nothing outside of him. The only thing that I find in my heart which disputes with Jesus the total possession of what is his, is a certain vague love of myself, a certain tendency to seek myself almost unconsciously: my well-being and my honor.

Thanks be to God I do not find in this respect anything deliberate; but the indeliberate, the hidden, in the subconsciousness, as we now say, reveals what we are: "Charity is not self-seeking." The love of Jesus should fill my heart completely. My love should be pure and disinterested.

Farther on he speaks of his miseries and says:

I saw a remarkable grace in God's permission regarding those miseries, because they have been the guarantee of my humility, the basis of my spiritual life and the indispensable condition for receiving God's graces and fulfilling a divine mission.

Some persons who half know me, exalt me for what I say and for what I do. Although I should like to believe what they tell me, I cannot; the counterweight of my miseries has me fastened in the cavern of my lowliness. Neither anything nor anyone can raise me."

Is not this a confirmation in humility, since we see how unable he was even to conceive a sentiment contrary to this virtue? It is not the simple virtue of humility, but humility exercised under the influence of the gifts, especially the gifts of fear of the Lord, knowledge and understanding. It is the gift of humility. He proceeds:

What would become of me without my miseries? With the Psalmist I ought to say: "It is good that thou hast humbled me!"

I must continue asking God, as I once did, to do with me what he wishes, to give me what pleases him, to accomplish through me the marvels he desires; but not to take away my tatters! Let him live in me underneath them!

In another place he writes the following, which is more directly pertinent to our subject.

In those exercises, the second resolution is this: to resemble Jesus: (a) through purity; (b) through humility, not admitting anything contrary to purity and striving for the greatest purity of intention in all my actions, especially in the ministry.

In another place he writes:

I ought to love Jesus with a true, deep, perfect love as far as it is possible to my limitations. I ought, therefore, to eliminate my egoism, to forget myself, not to seek myself, to efface myself.

Later, upon formulating his resolutions, he says:

Consequently, to solve all my problems, I need two things: to forget myself completely and to love Jesus with a love that is a total consecration of myself to him. In order not to seek myself, I need to seek Jesus in everything and through everything. Not to desire to please myself nor to please any creature: neither superiors, nor brethren, nor subjects, but only Jesus.

This desire to give him pleasure in everything, in each act, at each instant, nourished in prayer, will realize the ideal of love which is a definitive and total consecration.

In the retreat of 1941, God revealed to him a new way of loving him, a new love. He calls it the precious pearl which, once one knows about it, he must go and sell all to buy it:

But—can it be boldness?—I feel in my innermost soul that I do not need to buy that love, that I possess it. The graces of 1927 united me in truth to Jesus, and all my deficiencies and vicissitudes have not been sufficient to obliterate the divine reality of those graces.

In regard to the *new love*, when Jesus revealed it to me, did he not give me possession of himself? But it is evident I need to preserve and develop that treasure. For that I need prayer. He who gave me the light and the desire, will give me the gift and he will preserve it. On my part it occurs to me that it is necessary to work and to forget myself in order to love Jesus in a new way. There is urgent need of a work of relinquishing, forgetting, annihilating the *ego*.

Yet without denying the importance and the efficacy of this proceeding, I think that perfect forgetfulness of ourselves is not obtained by constant and methodical exercise in forgetting ourselves, but only by such an intense, absorbing love, that it does not allow us to think about ourselves. One can reach ordinary forgetfulness by the road of oblivion; one reaches perfect forgetfulness only through the pathway of love.

But incredibly, however alarming, however absurd this may appear, here is the sad reality: the great enemy of love is egoism, that stupid, incurable eagerness to seek ourselves. How much I have striven in my life to tear that enemy of love out of my heart! And when I have believed that now my heart is free from it, I discover again the humiliating traces of egoism! In a concealed, ingenious, subtle way, here is the enemy in my desires, in my sufferings, in my words.

I have always seen two kinds of motives for being humble: one which is based on truth; and the other on love. Now I see that the first kind refers to humility as a special virtue, whereas the second touches it in its intimate relations with love.

To cultivate humility, I must habitually consider those two motives, especially those of the second class; analyze carefully my thoughts, intentions, words, so that sneaky self-love may not hide in them and also to combat it when discovered; and finally, to make a particular examen upon humility.

In that struggle against egoism, he analyzes so minutely that he discovers a new form of egoism:

It consists in giving myself pleasure in simple things, like reading or rest, things which in themselves are neither illicit nor dangerous, and which on occasions may be useful and even necessary, but which frequently are done to give myself pleasure.

One must combat egoism with discretion even in this regard. This kind of egoism produces disorder in occupations. Perhaps also, this form of egoism has relationship with that other subtle form which in the spiritual realm impels us to seek consolations with excess. For Jesus to live fully in me, I must disappear completely.

In the retreat of 1945, the chief resolution is: "That our mutual love may be my felicity, that Jesus may be my all and my only one. To this end I wish to forget myself entirely; I will make my particular examen upon admitting nothing of self-love."

In the "practical rules" of the retreat of 1947, he insists: "Egoism is the only enemy of love." And the second of the resolutions is to devote the particular examen "upon not speaking of myself in what may be favorable to me and unnecessary to say. The aforesaid examen will be extended to the whole subject of humility if advisable."

In the retreat of 1950, the fourth resolution is: "To try not to speak well of myself, except when it might be necessary."

In that of 1951, the fourth resolution: "I will make the particular examen upon this point: Not to seek myself. In all things I will try to preserve myself in humility."

Through this ingenuous and sincere confession which he makes in his diary, one guesses what a degree of perfection he attained in humility: "Lately I have felt an interior joy in humbling myself and disappearing; it is not something reasoned out, but a kind of inspiration, a sweet, esthetic intuition of humility, without knowing why."

But we could continue interminably. For the Archbishop, humility and love are basically one same reality. They are like the positive and the negative aspect of one and the same thing.

I knew Archbishop Martínez before he was a priest: he was then of a lively temperament. As prefect of discipline at the Institute he used to watch the study hall. One day a student talking with another, was told to keep silence; again another time, without result. When the prefect ordered him to leave the hall, the student did not obey; then the prefect caught the offender under the shoulders and almost bodily pulled him out of the hall to force him to obey.

Nevertheless, he gradually acquired so perfect a meekness that when on some rare occasion he was obliged to reprehend energetically, he had to feign an annoyance that he was far from feeling.

On one occasion, when a person rebelled against his authority, the Archbishop was obliged to assert it energetically. When this mishap passed, someone offered him a tranquilizer. Smiling gratefully, he declined it and said with ingenuity: "I did not feel the least disturbance within me. Everything was exterior and forced by necessity."

In the same way we might continue discussing the other virtues of Christ, reproduced in Archbishop Martínez, insofar as human limitations permit it. There was his obedience to ecclesiastical and divine laws and a submission to all the manifestations of the divine will until his love for that will became a real passion. Like Jesus, he was distinguished by his indulgence, kindness, charity for all without distinction, whereby he conquered all hearts.

In regard to charity, this feature alone proves it: never was he heard to speak ill of anyone, neither of the rulers—frequently the target of all blame—nor of his brethren in the episcopate, nor of his inferiors. Especially was he jealous in guarding the reputation of his priests.

Charity for one's neighbor is an essential element, although secondary, of Christian perfection. Through the intimate union which we have with Jesus as members of the Mystical Body and, therefore, partakers of the divine, there is an intimate connection between charity toward God and charity toward the neighbor. "What you do to one of my little ones you do to me," says Jesus.

What a satisfaction it is to be able to pay Jesus, in the neighbor, although it may be little, for what he does for us. The love of neighbor marvelously complements the love of God.

But if whatever we do for the neighbor is precious because we are doing it for Jesus, the most precious thing in charity is to do spiritual good to souls. Zeal for the salvation of souls is the essential duty of every Christian, but especially of the priest and of the bishop. To us belongs something of what Jesus said to Peter: "Do you love me, Peter, more than these? ... Feed my lambs."

To fulfill this duty, the first and essential thing is the love of Jesus, for St. Thomas teaches that the apostolic life is the overflowing of the interior life. For us, to feed the lambs of Jesus is the overflowing of that episcopal and sacerdotal love that Jesus thus expresses: "Do you love me more than these?"

Jesus made me perceive this truth in a special way, more through his interior communication than through reasoning.

In the second place, His Excellency reproduced mystically the mysteries of Jesus. The soul that has been transformed into Christ lives the life of Christ. Is not this the essence of the transformation?

To live the life of Christ is nothing else than to reproduce his mysteries. The mysteries of Christ's life, as historic facts, are past; but as dispositions of the soul of Jesus, they have not passed; Christ preserves them in the Eucharist and he preserves them in heaven. Those interior dispositions of the heart of Christ are the soul, the essence, the interior of all his mysteries.

In a special way, Archbishop Martínez reproduced the mystery of Bethlehem and the mystery of Calvary, which are the alpha and the omega of the life of Christ and the compendium of all his mysteries.

The model of these virtues, or rather the models, are in the cave of Bethlehem. What a mystery of poverty in the Child! "For you know the graciousness of our Lord Jesus Christ—how being rich, he became poor for your sakes, that by his poverty you might become rich" (II Cor. 8:9). How could the one who is infinitely rich by nature become poor, and so poor?

Poor, most poor, are Joseph and Mary, who did not find in the dwellings of men a little corner where Jesus might be born. But what is most beautiful and sublime is the perfect forgetfulness of themselves of these three persons in this celestial idyll of Bethlehem.

Mary, after the heavenly night, and before no doubt, lived in an ecstasy of divine love; not in those ecstacies that suspend the senses, but in those that draw out the soul and imprison it in the beloved being, for, as St. Denis said, "Divine love causes ecstasy." How could that blessed Mother who saw her God in her little Son, think about herself?

Joseph participated in that ecstasy, but with the singular prerogative that it did not hinder him from attending to the necessities of life for the Holy Family; as neither did it stop the Virgin from her domestic tasks, since the occupations of both had their center and their unity in the divine Child.

But the most wonderful thing is the self-forgetfulness of Jesus. It seems that he could not, that he should not forget himself. We forget ourselves, because we are nothing, to think about God. But, how can Jesus, who is God, forget himself?

St. Alphonsus Liguori has explained this doctrine in masterly fashion: "For love of us he became man and he chose for himself a life of suffering and the death of the cross; and he preferred our happiness to his own honor, his own comfort, and his own life, renouncing everything to show us his love."

Thus I ought to live in an ecstasy of love which might envelop in its unity all my occupations which, thanks be to God, have Jesus as their center and unity.

To live that way, one needs to be disposed to suffer, or rather, to look deeply into suffering and to love it sincerely. How many times we break off contemplation and love because we avoid a sacrifice, become disquieted by a contradiction, or fail to find in sorrow the secret of peace and of perfect joy!

Archbishop Martínez realized this ideal in his life. Few souls have entered so far within the spirit of spiritual infancy. He assimilated the "spirit of adoption" and with the Son he cried out to the Father: "Abba, Father!" He loved the Son with a reflection of the love of Mary and Joseph. His heart was a perpetual Bethlehem.

But he also reproduced the mystery of Calvary. This constitutes the third mission of His Excellency, which was to be a victim with Jesus, which we shall see in the following chapter.

In the third place the Archbishop did the work of Jesus. Monsignor Gay has a precious thought: "To do the work of Jesus it is necessary to be Jesus." But it can also be stated: "He who is Jesus does the work of Jesus."

Archbishop Martínez, transformed into Jesus, did the work of Jesus; that is to say, he was a true apostle. As he says:

It is not enough for the apostle to speak, to work, to anticipate all those forms of human activity. The apostle must communicate God even in inactivity and silence, by a wonderful spiritual fecundity.

As one who carries with him a handful of fragrant flowers does not need to spray the atmosphere nor speak nor do anything, but simply be there; so the apostle, full of God (transformed into Jesus), does not need to do anything else to communicate him but approach souls; for where he passes, he will leave everything imbued with the good odor of Christ.

The more pure, the more loving, the more contemplative, the more sacrificing the apostle, the more perfectly will he possess this spiritual fecundity. Replica of Mary, the apostle will carry Jesus and he will give Jesus, always and everywhere, as Mary carries him and gives him.

On another occasion he writes:

Another grace of our Lord which I ought to acknowledge with full optimism is that my heart has expanded and charity for my neighbor increased in it, a virtue eminently sacerdotal. No one imagines how I love souls, how I should like to sacrifice myself for them, how happy I am with their happiness. During the retreat at...the Superior admitted to me that more than what I preached or said to her personally, it was the charity, patience and sweetness with which I treated everyone that had done her good.

Some time afterwards he says:

Our Lord has given me during this last season, the perfect joy of the apostolate; how greatly souls make me rejoice! And suffer, too ... although less. Many times I have felt a strength for supporting and consoling souls as if I apparently needed neither support nor comfort. Our Lord has made me see that he constitutes my strength to support and console, and that I need no other comfort and support than he, who is intimately united with my soul. In certain seasons I feel neither the sweetness nor the fervor of union; but the peace, the strength and a kind of solidity and intimacy that I experience give testimony to that most blessed union.

Afterwards I noted the martyrdom and the felicity of love for the neighbor, for one suffers the griefs and enjoys the happiness of others. How Jesus, father of all souls, must have suffered and rejoiced!

Elsewhere he writes that, in order to make the ministry a ladder to go to Jesus, it is necessary "to live with him, to live through him, to live in him."

To do everything *with him,* with the consciousness that he is present in my soul, that he does everything with me, that we both always live as one, because my life is fused with his life.

To do everything *through him,* through love. No motive lower than this is worthy of a soul united to Jesus, of a sacerdotal soul. Everything done through love bears us to Jesus and tightens our bond with him.

To live *in him,* that is, to see everything with his eyes, to feel with his heart, to work with his spirit. Faith and love transfigure everything and divinize it.

The second way for Jesus to live in me is by my renewing his life and his mysteries in my life. Each spiritual life, and especially the priest's life, should be a reproduction, a copy of Jesus' life. How inspiring that Jesus continues to live in us and to accomplish his designs! How consoling that he does his work in us! I asked him

for this and he promised it to me when I accepted the archbishopric.

The expression of St. Paul must be realized in me: "Let this
sentiment be in you which is in Christ Jesus." May his thoughts be
my thoughts; his affections, my affections; his life-giving impulse
be mine.

For the first, I ought to judge of everything supernaturally, "to
see through the eyes of Jesus." Especially in God's work, which I
must do, it is necessary to see the divine. Perhaps in the surroundings in which God has placed me there is a special tendency to see
humanly; greater reason to work divinely. I ought to eliminate
carefully human reasons and a human way of proceeding; this is a
new elimination of the *ego*.

Looking at everything through Jesus' eyes, that is, according to
his judgment and according to his Spirit, he will live in me, my
life will be a reproduction of his life. But to supernatural discernment one must add supernatural love, since light and love perform
the work. The love of Jesus, his priestly love, the love of the Father
and the love of souls, must be the love of my heart, the life of my
life.

We could continue indefinitely, but it is necessary to stop.
For a conclusion let us reproduce two scenes which show us
graphically how Archbishop Martínez was another Christ.

A few days ago, while travelling from one town to another, I
arrived at the shore of the Lerma River. Hundreds or perhaps
thousands of persons accompanied me to the beach, shouting,
"Long live Christ the King!" It was about nine at night, the sky
was glorious, the stars scintillating and the moon illuminating the
scene. That whole multitude covered the shore which, on account
of its particular topography, permitted a view at one glance of that
entire people; music playing, men cheering, and skyrockets shoot-
ing into the air.

I entered a boat to pass to the other shore; naturally I was enjoying the poetry of that scene. But upon recalling that passage of
the Gospel which tells that Jesus spoke to the multitudes from a

boat pulling away from the shore, I so felt that scene on Tiberias there in the scent on the Lerma, that I experienced a deep, very sweet impression, but an insupportable one.

Ah, Jesus was right in hiding himself from us in this life! With the light that the Holy Spirit diffuses in our understanding and with the love which he pours out into our hearts, we cannot support Jesus except veiled, hidden; our weakness is not able to resist if the veil is raised just a little.

Here is another scene, years later:

One day I was visiting a village in the suburbs of Mexico City; the people surrounded me, throwing flowers and confetti, kissing my ring, pushing me around affectionately. A man of the village said: "Our Lord must be like that!" Only God knows what I felt and what that ingenuous expression suggested to me.

I want him to be seen through me, not so much to love and protect me, as to work and do good by means of me.

CHAPTER IX

Victim With Jesus

TO BE VICTIM with Jesus was the third mission of Archbishop Martínez. We shall see presently how the three missions are fulfilled mutually, for *to sacrifice himself* was substantially the work of Jesus and, as we have seen, to do Jesus' work, it is necessary to have been transformed into him and *to be a living portrait of Christ.* But no soul can be transformed into Christ *without exhibiting the divine love,* as much because this transformation is the work of love as because, if our Lord came to acquaint us with divine love and to accommodate it to our smallness, every soul transformed into him is necessarily proclaiming that love continually.

Just as little St. Thérèse hid a whole life of suffering under a smile, similarly, the good humor, the jovial manner, the ever-festive character concealed in the Archbishop the great sufferings with which our Lord developed his soul to maturity, to that maturity which suffering alone can give.

He was born practically an orphan. His cradle was covered with crepe eleven days after his birth, when his father died. He found an adoptive father in a maternal uncle, a priest; but he died when the boy was seven years old and for a second time he became an orphan. Another maternal uncle adopted him, but he also died when Archbishop Martínez was still a young priest.

As his spiritual father, he recognized Bishop Banegas, to whom he owed the orientation of his intelligence, the formation of his character, in great part, and the cultivation of his endowments as sacred orator and writer. But he also died. In his personal notes Archbishop Martínez writes:

On the days preceding the death of Bishop Banegas, God enveloped me in tenderness and peace as it always happens when our Lord is going to give me a sorrow. But who would believe that I "felt" with our Lord? I can almost assert that I had never "felt" with anyone, and I have even said many times that any shade of sensibility which is neither annoyance nor content does not fit into my sensibility; but now I certainly was affected. After Bishop Banegas died, I could not contact Jesus without weeping and without an emotional state I had not experienced before. Can it be a certain loving resentment? Or can it be that when we approach a loved person the pain in our soul comes to the surface? I believe that there was something of the one and of the other. Especially during the Mass that I sang in the cathedral, tears gushed from my eyes, and from my soul flowed something between bitterness and sweetness.

Of course I accepted completely God's will and even gave him thanks; but I also had my struggles.

These lines give us some idea of how much he loved Bishop Banegas.

Very close bonds also united him with Archbishop Leopoldo Ruiz. They understood each other admirably; there was in them a full mutual confidence and an affection which had much of the filial in Archbishop Martínez and of the paternal in Archbishop Ruiz. In a personal letter he writes:

You already know of the death of Archbishop Ruiz and you can imagine what I have felt, for you know well that he was a father to me. He died as he had lived, with love, with serenity, and above all with that simplicity which characterized him.

I had the consolation of visiting him in his illness, of recommending his soul, singing his funeral Mass and accompanying his mortal remains to the tomb. I went to the solemn rites in Morelia on January 14 and I preached the sermon.

He died on December 12 (1941), and this makes me think

that on that same day he entered heaven, for it seems to me unbecoming and incongruous that the Blessed Virgin could have taken him on that day to purgatory. On the other hand, his holy life makes me hope for that same thing; his human failings were excesses of kindness.

Before Archbishop Ruiz' death and afterwards he had to lament successively the loss of his friends and companions, especially Canon E. Reyes and Canon J. B. Buitrón. With the latter, especially, he shared a very intimate friendship, treating him with utmost confidence. He loved him so much, as His Excellency confessed to me, that although he had courage to attend all his loved ones, he did not feel the fortitude to accompany Canon Buitrón at the end.

But no loss can be compared with what he suffered at the death of his mother. As I have indicated before, I have never known a son and a mother who loved each other so greatly. I cannot resist the desire of reproducing here two intimate letters in which he refers to his sorrow:

Her death was very sweet and it left in my soul satisfaction and peace. Since October of the past year I have the happiness of keeping in my oratory the Blessed Sacrament and since then my mother spent the days at the foot of the altar asking especially for the grace of a holy death. God granted it to her completely, to such a degree that death never seemed so sweet to me as when I saw her die.

From January first, I was absent from the city on the pastoral visits to the parishes, which is one of my principal obligations, and I intended to return to this city the fourteenth of February. My mother came to see me at Maravatío and spent three days with me, in better health and more cheerful than ever. She had just returned from Maravatío when she became ill with the grippe. Without knowing of her sickness, I providentially arrived in this city on the fifth of February through the kindness of the Archbishop who, fearing that I might become ill from the work of the visitation, made me come; and God, as always, made use of the obedience to accomplish his designs.

I had scarcely arrived when my mother's condition became more serious and God gave me immediately full confidence that he would cure her, if it was his will, and an absolute conformity to his good pleasure if he ordained her death.

Very soon I understood what was the will of God; on Sunday, the eighth, her illness was declared bronchial pneumonia and I lost all hope. That day I myself had the consolation of administering the sacraments of the Viaticum and Extreme Unction, which she received with entire simplicity and singular devotion, answering clearly all the questions of the Ritual.

I asked her afterwards how the visit of Jesus had gone with her, and she answered me: "Lovely little secrets." After the sacraments she said to the persons attending her that she no longer wanted anything of this world; afterwards she took nourishment and medicine only through deference and because I told her it was God's will.

During the night from Sunday to Monday, I asked her if she was taking medicine, and she answered that she was not. "Do you want me to grant you the plenary indulgence?" That, indeed. She pronounced the name of Jesus three times, with a devotion that filled me with consolation, and then I asked her: "Do you conform yourself to the will of God in all the sufferings and discomforts of your sickness and even to death itself?" She answered me with heartfelt accents that I shall never forget: "Yes, even to death itself."

She accepted death with a complete, loving conformity to God's will. During that night, all Monday and during the night from Monday to Tuesday, I approached her bed from time to time, exhorting her to resignation and confidence. I spoke to her of Jesus, of the Virgin Mary, of heaven. She always listened to me with deep gratitude. Sometimes she was visibly moved, and she constantly kissed the crucifix that she always held in her hand. No uneasiness, not a glance at the things of this world; her spirit was oriented toward eternity.

They brought her a statue of little St. Thérèse; she took it with both hands and asked the saint to take her soon to heaven. Many times I prayed the recommendation of a departing soul, accompanied almost always by several priests. On all these times, even the last, she herself gave the responses and she repeated the ejaculations which I suggested to her, even correcting me when I made a mistake; for God gave her the grace of not losing consciousness for an instant in spite of the high temperatures.

On Monday and on Tuesday, at daybreak, she again received the Viaticum; and one hour before her death she heard the Mass that I celebrated opposite her bed; and she heard it with great devotion, striking her breast at the time of consecration and making the Sign of the Cross at the blessing. Her last contact with this world, as final proof of her maternal tenderness (so immense during her life!) was to tell the persons caring for her, at the end of the Mass, to give me breakfast. A half hour later, she died easily with her eyes fixed on heaven.

Her death impregnated me with sweetness, with peace and almost with joy. God has filled me with consolations and graces. Why does God treat me thus? I had scarcely closed her eyes when I went to the oratory to pray in the midst of tears a *Te Deum* in thanksgiving for the years which he gave her to me, in thanksgiving because he took her away from me, in thanksgiving for that holy death.

I had the consolation of singing her Requiem Mass myself, of accompanying her to the cemetery, of blessing her tomb, of chanting the absolution at the grave, of throwing upon her dear remains the first handful of earth and of saying to her full of hope: *Until tomorrow!*

My composure attracted the attention of some, because they did not know that there within God was pouring copiously his strength, his sweetness and his comfort.

How much I have learned these days! No doubt I remain alone in the world without that warmth, without that very special tenderness with which her maternal heart always surrounded me; but, she is already happy or will be so very soon! And in the eyes of our faith and in the security of our hope, what is lacking, as we look forward to that *tomorrow* which will reunite us all in peace, in the joy of eternal brightness?

I know that now my mother loves me more and loves me better than on earth, because she loves me in truth, in order, in the fatherland of love, in the bosom of God. She will care for me and help me better than before (I have experienced it already!) and she will be more united than ever with me, because death does not separate, it *unites* souls. Between my mother's soul and mine there is no longer anything but God, and God is the *least* and the *most* that there can be between souls, isn't that so? What is lacking to me of tenderness and sensible joy will help to break all earthly bonds, to die to all that is human, to give myself up wholly to God. Ask him that it may be so, that I also may die completely so that my life may be hidden with Christ in God, and in that welcome hiddenness find the beloved soul of my mother.

How much I should like to talk with you. But this letter has been prolonged excessively. The need—and the difficulty—of confidence is never felt as on these occasions.

Help me to thank God and intercede for the release of my mother's soul from purgatory without delay. I have great hope that she is now in heaven: her simple, pious life, her holy death, the innumerable suffrages, and above all, the goodness of God toward me; but who knows the judgments of God?

Yours affectionately in the divine heart of Christ. . . ."

Our Lord softened the first blow, but the reaction came later. This can be explained even humanly: a mighty sorrow seems to crush us and blunt our sensibility; but when the first impression passes, we begin little by little to muse over our suffering, then it becomes bitter and desolate. Let us notice this in another letter of the Archbishop written four months after his mother's death.

If you only knew how much good the simple narration of your present life did for me! I read it when my human life was crumbling into a cataclysm and your letter showed me—what Jesus already taught me interiorly—the true value of life.

I thought myself very detached from this world, but the death of my mother showed me the hidden bonds that joined me to life, which that death came to break. How certain it is that nature, exterior things, are but the stage upon which man moves, the nest which guards love!

In order to understand what follows, let us take into account that Ramoncita loved birds and flowers. Her house was full of flowers and of birds which she herself cared for; not only because she liked them, but especially for her son so that he might find his home happy and cheerful.

When spring began to touch the earth with its warm, fragrant caress, when the flowers in the sunny patio began to open up, those flowers my dear mother used to cultivate so lovingly, and the birds which she loved and cared for began their once happy songs, I felt bad, very bad and I understood that for me life had been changed, that implacable death had torn love from my existence, because I loved her, and I loved her for *herself*.

Impelled by my egoism, I saw death as a hope, and I felt a horror for life, for the years ahead, long, interminable, desolate . . . and I sighed for the silence of a cloister.

But that impression was passing; yet it has been renewed many times. My mother was not the reason of my life; the reason of my life is Jesus and I ought to have the strength to live for him and through him. Earthly life ended for me and I should never revive it.

Life is an affection around which everything turns. Thank God I no longer have any earthly affection and in him I hope never to have it. Earthly life is finished for me; I died with my mother.

But a new life should begin for me with another light, another love, with other desires; just as a new life has commenced for my mother. I shall live with her, by seeing—above all earthly things which have passed for her and for me—what she sees; seeing it in the light of faith, each day purer, clearer, deeper; by loving what she loves, loving it with that supernatural love which the Holy

Spirit has poured into my soul, and which each day should be more ardent, more pure and disinterested; touching through hope what she touches by possession.

Your letter showed me how in the tedious monotony of colorless days and in the torturing anguish of evil times, victorious, beautifying love can be hidden to give life its value and its charm.

With the death of my mother, God has wrought marvels in my soul; he has detached me from everything, and he has put his love so deeply into my heart, that all my ingratitude and my wretchedness will not succeed in tearing it out of there.

The Archbishop survived his mother exactly thirty-one years but his heartfelt love for her remained intact, and her memory, at once so sweet and so bitter, was ever a thorn in his heart. An evidence of this is that in his last agony, in that unconscious state in which deep thoughts come up to the lips, he called out several times: "Mama! Mama!" just as a child might have done.

Later on, Señora Armida, with whose soul he had such supernatural ties, passed from this life; then an aunt, who had continued keeping house for him after the death of his mother and who had always lived with her. In 1947 he wrote:

The other light which I received a few days ago, inundated my spirit, in considering the behavior of our Lord toward me lately. He has kept on taking away from me all that could serve me as support and comfort. He took Angela (his aunt) away and left me without family ties; he took away X, a learned, great-souled man, a very close friend who helped me with his advice and upon whom I relied in all business matters.

In a new way I understood that he desires to be my only one and my all. He is enough for me; for me he is family, counsellor, loved one. I ought to delve into these depths: He, *all!* There is nothing which my heart cannot find in him. He, alone! He suffices for me, I do not need anyone.

Of course, so far as he may wish, I can find light, friendship, joy, in creatures, but in him and through him; and absolutely speaking,

I do not need them, it is enough for me to be with him. But it is urgent that I learn to treat Jesus—the infinite adapted to my smallness—in a new, deep, sweet way; that I learn to listen to him, to unite myself with him. I must learn to trust him fully and to seek and to find all that I need and desire in him. In this way life is simplified and elevated.

Between jests and truths, I have said that this world is made up of "little bits." In fact, how many articles of clothing to dress oneself! How much variety, how many actions each day! The most excellent things we have, knowledge and love, need many little pieces. Our knowledge is formed of complicated reasonings; each reasoning, of several judgments; each judgment, of several ideas. And to fill the heart, a series of varied and unrequited affections. ...Life is simplified in unity with Jesus.

But how sorrowful is the road that takes the soul to that solitude!

In his final years, the Archbishop wrote:

When one begins to see what one loves, he sighs for the full possession of heaven and of that land which, according to St. John of the Cross, "knows eternal life." The soul also feels the driving necessity of giving itself, of seeking, of doing the will of the Beloved and of being satisfied in it.

But I see another high step on the ladder of love, one where everything disappears, even the one who loves, and only the Beloved remains, filling everything. "For me, to live is Christ." Then the divine solitude, of which I spoke in my letter, must be experienced.

The newly married, when they have taken leave of their guests, exclaim: "Alone at last!" Love sighs for this solitude to have full expression. With greater reason divine love desires this divine solitude; for in the plenitude of love, creatures are in the way, and in that solitude is realized the phrase in the Canticle: "My Beloved for me and I for my Beloved." When everything is a hindrance, when the Beloved is sufficient, one has reached the summit of love: it is the heavenly solitude of those who love.

God, no doubt, lets me see these heights so as to conduct souls toward them, and also to enkindle in my own soul the desire of ascending and of making all sacrifices necessary for such a height.

To leave all to him, to glimpse the beauty of the Beloved, to give myself up to love without reserve! This is the foundation of the true life; it is eternal life. Without Jesus, life would be intolerable; with him, even death is sweet. For to me to live is Christ and to die is gain.

There is no doubt but that the path of Archbishop Martínez was bordered with tombs and shaded with cypresses. These separations, which tore his sensitive heart, remained hidden under the veil of his incurable joviality.

Let us enumerate a few more of his sufferings. These always included voluntary mortification. He used the traditional instruments of penance, such as disciplines, hair shirts, fasts and vigils (he chose midnight as the principal time for prayer and called his nights "delightful").

According to his doctrine, suffering has three stages: first, it purifies; afterwards, it resembles Jesus Crucified; finally, it contributes to the salvation of souls. *The suffering that purifies, the suffering that unites, the suffering that saves.* Through these three stages he passed successively.

We have seen something of passive purifications. In his work, *Only Jesus,* we can read his beautiful pages on the transformation of the soul into Jesus Crucified, the fruit of his own experience. In his later years he wrote:

Suffering is needed for the apostolate. Detachment, the necessary condition of love, requires it; but it is also the secret of the apostolate, because it is the secret of fecundity. The sufferings of the apostolate are bodily fatigue, misunderstanding and other sacrifices in dealing with the neighbor, and immolation from penance.

When some problem of souls or of the government of the diocese is perplexing, some special sacrifice must be offered. There are demons that cannot be expelled except by prayer and penance. There are graces that cannot be attained except through sacrifice added to prayer.

Our apostolic methods should be those of Jesus: his ineffable way of treating souls: energy and sweetness, humility and meekness. One must become all to all to gain all for Christ.

How well he portrays himself in those words!

"Perfect joy," he writes, "breaks forth from sorrow. To suffer for Jesus and for souls, to share in the priestly sorrows of Jesus, to show him our love with our sufferings, to buy with them happiness for souls! . . . Can a more solid, more exquisite, more fruitful joy be given?"

One of the great sacrifices of his life was his episcopal work, arduous, crushing, and, if we had not been witness of it, incredible. Humanly he could not have withstood it for thirty-two years without a grace which we might qualify as extraordinary.

In his pastoral ministry he showed a truly heroic patience: in those long hours of conference, with so many impertinent persons, whom he received with the utmost kindness, without hurry, as if the person whom he was receiving were the only one to whom he had to attend; in those interminable series of confirmations, in a suffocating atmosphere, in the midst of the crying of hundreds of children; in his constant trips in which he had to adapt himself to the discomforts of the lodging, the diversity of foods, the variety of climate and the like.

On one occasion someone asked him: "Your Excellency, is your bed uncomfortable?" And he answered with his customary readiness: "Which one?" He varied his bed so frequently, that his own might be considered as one of many; therefore he asked in his turn which bed of the many he used could be uncomfortable.

In spite of the fact that he suffered from indigestion, he always accepted whatever they served him, never asking for special foods. To conceal his mortification he used to say: "I have an international stomach."

In his final years Archbishop Martínez endured two classes

of sufferings which were the last touches with which our Lord finished his masterpiece. Of the first we can say little, discretion and prudence forbid it. Almost always the greatest sufferings with which God finishes the sanctification of a soul are wounds caused by beloved hands. But in this case there is something that reaches the final summit of heroism: His Excellency not only did not open his lips to defend himself; not only did he forbid a single word to be said in his defense, but he denied himself the lawful consolation of an unburdening. To no one, *absolutely no one,* did he say a word about his sufferings, not even to his most intimate friends, not even under rigid secrecy. All these sufferings, all the humiliations which they brought with them, he suffered in a divinely heroic silence.

The other class of sufferings came with his last illness, initiated some two years before. He came to Mexico City in the maturity of his spirit and the fullness of his strength. In September, 1944, he writes: "During the past month two excellent physicians, my ordinary doctor and a heart specialist, saw me and they saw me again with X-rays. They examined me with some wonderful apparatus. Their opinion was that I could live twenty years more; that in the heart and the whole circulatory system I have absolutely no bad symptoms; that in the lungs I have nothing serious, but something in the bronchial tubes on account of age, preaching (forty-one years!) and tobacco."[1]

Nevertheless, instead of twenty years more, he survived only

---

[1] The Archbishop was a great smoker; during the day he smoked cigarettes in an unlimited number, besides a cigar after the midday meal. In 1930, he realized that our Lord wanted him to limit the use of tobacco. "I do not suppress it all," he writes, "because I fear losing nervous equilibrium, which, if it is necessary for all, is indispensable for superiors. As tobacco has a special action on the nervous system, its sudden suppression (in those accustomed to it) can destroy that equilibrium." In 1932, he writes: "In regard to tobacco, I am going very slowly: I smoke eight cigarettes daily; sometimes I increase it by one. The cigars are very rare." Soon he discontinued the cigar for the rest of his life and limited the cigarettes to four a day.

half of that. Excess of work and moral sufferings felled that mighty oak. Alarmed, the physicians prescribed absolute rest. Soon he completely lost the sight of his right eye and could see only a little with the left eye. He also began to lose hearing and memory; and he walked with difficulty because of varicose veins. Physically, he was completely broken.

One day, hoping to encourage him, we recalled to him an anecdote about Lacordaire. In his last days, while addressing his students, the eloquent orator of Notre Dame began to stammer. Some of the young men, with the thoughtlessness of youth, could not restrain their laughter. Then Lacordaire silenced them with the words: "Yes, my friends, my sword is dulled; but it has been in your service!" His Excellency smiled, understanding the allusion. His sword was dulled in the mighty service of God and of souls.

How many hours, how many days of solitude, with neither visitors, nor reading, nor business affairs, nor spiritual ministrations, nor anything. On August 6, 1954, in Jiménez, Chihuahua, he preached his last sermon at a sacerdotal jubilee.

During the last days, a very intimate friend, seeing him sad and depressed, contrary to his custom, dared to say: "Your Excellency, do you suffer much?"

Recovering his habitual affability, he answered with ingenuous sincerity: "You see I don't! I love the will of God too much! ... My soul is so full of peace!"

On Thursday, February 1, 1956, he celebrated his last Mass; he could scarcely finish it. The intestinal hemorrhages, which had already begun days before, were aggravated.

They conducted him to his bed. A series of blood transfusions, serum injections and other treatments followed. That same day, at midnight, his confessor was called, because the seriousness increased. Nevertheless, accustomed to those illnesses from which his vigorous constitution rallied, no one thought that the end was near.

The night of the first Friday, February 2, Monsignor Ruiz Solórzano and the Archbishop's confessor decided, under the urgent circumstances, to administer the last sacraments, without waiting for the following day. It was necessary, therefore, to prescind from the solemnity with which this rite is carried out customarily in the case of a prelate.

Monsignor Ruiz was charged with giving the Archbishop the notification of his approaching death. He did so with composure, without circumlocutions. His Excellency received the news with the same composure and with a naturalness and serenity not always found even in saintly souls.

What a picture in simplicity! The narrow bedroom of a dying man, illuminated by the light of two wax tapers. The personages, Monsignor Ruiz, the confessor and bosom friend of the Archbishop and some few intimate persons. The group did not even fill the room.

Monsignor Ruiz, with the sacred host in his hands—the last Communion of the Archbishop—asks him the questions of the Ritual of Toledo. The dying man answers with a firm, sonorous voice that we had not heard for a long time: "I do believe! . . . I do ask pardon! . . . I do pardon! . . ."

Afterwards, the anointing . . . then, the silence of thanksgiving.

The doctors exhausted all the resources of science and succeeded in prolonging a life, already unconscious, until the dawn of Thursday.

When the measure of suffering was filled up, God accepted the victim: "Enter into the joy of thy Lord!" And the soul of Archbishop Martínez went to be submerged in the ocean of infinite love.

Epilogue

THE DEATH of Archbishop Martínez was changed into a true apotheosis. From dawn of Thursday, February ninth, until the evening of Saturday, February eleventh, day and night, thousands and thousands of the faithful filed before his mortal remains. That evening his casket was placed in the crypt of the altar of the Kings, but the crypt had to be opened again so that the interminable line might pass by. It is not an exaggeration to calculate that a million persons have visited the mortal remains of Archbishop Martínez.

The Holy See, the President of the Republic, the diplomatic corps, numerous foreign nations, including Israel, presented their condolences; but above all, the more lowly people, with tears as sincere as spontaneous, bedewed the mortal remains of the one who for them was a true father.

The highest ranking prelates of the nation and even some from distant countries gathered for the rites. Cardinal Spellman came from New York expressly and of his own accord to preside at the funeral.

In brief, no one recalls that in the entire history of Mexico was there ever a case of similar grief. Therefore, it can be affirmed that it was a sorrow not circumscribed by the Archdiocese of Mexico City, not even by the nation, but one that went beyond our borders and moved the Catholic world. Condolences were received from all over the world.

On April 14, 1937, the main door of the cathedral of Mexico City had opened wide for the entrance of the new Archbishop of Mexico. He came from Morelia, fasting, in order to celebrate Mass after taking possession of his archdiocese.

217

When all the canonical prescriptions had been fulfilled, His Excellency ascended the pulpit to speak to his flock for the first time. The faithful filled the cathedral to capacity. Scarcely had he begun to speak when an unfortunate accident occurred. The wood floor, deteriorated by time, yielded to the weight of the multitude and caved in near the sanctuary on the Epistle side. The confusion and alarm were great, although the collapse had no consequences of importance; but the Archbishop's sermon was ruined.

When calm was restored, it seemed fitting to him to limit himself to these words: "I am here only to promise you one single thing: *I come to give you my life.*"

In truth, the whole episcopate of Archbishop Martínez was reduced to fulfilling that promise.

He came, as we saw, in the maturity of his life, with health perfect by all standards, with a vigorous disposition, with seemingly inexhaustible energy. And he gave himself to the task without stint or measure.

Canon Sáenz, who was very well acquainted with the Archbishop all his life, once said of him: "I know him very well. He is an excellent priest but he has one defect; he never knows how to say 'no' to anything."

He was giving us to understand that His Excellency never denied anyone a service. When Archbishop Martínez found it out, he commented with his proverbial good humor: "The worst of it is that I do not intend to correct that defect."

And it never was corrected. His day was completely filled, from rising time until one o'clock in the morning, when he retired. He administered confirmation to hundreds of thousands; in the City of Mexico alone he used to confirm some two thousand children weekly, apart from the confirmations during pastoral visitations. Consequently, it is not an exaggeration to state that he confirmed no fewer than two million faithful. Many a time on Saturday, when confirmations were most frequent, he arrived at his house for the midday meal at five or six o'clock in the evening.[1]

He visited his extensive archdiocese,[2] with varying climates, difficult communication and some towns little less than inaccessible, like Nanchititla, situated on the top of a steep mountain, which can be reached only on mule back. He administered baptism, matrimony and First Communion to anyone who asked him, rich or poor, acquaintance or stranger. He received all classes of persons, during long hours of the day. He preached without ceasing. In Lent he began his series of spiritual exercises with the week of Septuagesima and ended with the sermons of Holy Week. Sometimes he gave two series at the same time. I remember one Good Friday when he had no time to eat at all, because the Office and the sermons filled his entire day.

When he was already ill with the sickness that carried him to the grave, a simple priest of a distant diocese invited him to preach on a feast day. In spite of the long, difficult trip, and one of his attacks, he consented as always and went to preach.

He literally killed himself with his work. Granted his iron constitution, he should have reached, humanly speaking, an advanced age. But with his mode of life, it was impossible to hold out for a long time. The good shepherd gave his life for his sheep.

Therefore, upon contemplating the mortal remains of Archbishop Martínez, it seemed that we recalled his promise made nineteen years before, and we thought that he said to us, with the eloquence of his deeds: "I promised to give you my life . . . and now, you see, *I have fulfilled it!*"

---

[1] In Mexico, the principal meal is usually at midday.
[2] The archdiocese of Mexico has more than four million Catholics.